# ARIZONA
## HIGHWAYS

# SCENIC
# DRIVES

# 40 of Arizona's Best Back Roads

Edited by Robert Stieve
and Kelly Vaughn Kramer

Text: *Arizona Highways* Contributors
Editors: Robert Stieve and Kelly Vaughn Kramer
Copy Editor: Noah Austin
Photographs: *Arizona Highways* Contributors
Designer: Keith Whitney
Photo Editor: Jeff Kida
Maps: Kevin Kibsey

Library of Congress Control Number: 2014941239
ISBN: 978-0-9916228-3-2
First printing, 2014. Second printing, 2015. Printed in China.

Published by the Book Division of *Arizona Highways* magazine, a monthly publication of the Arizona Department of Transportation, 2039 W. Lewis Avenue, Phoenix, Arizona 85009.
Telephone: 602-712-2200
Website: www.arizonahighways.com

Publisher: Win Holden
Editor: Robert Stieve
Managing Editor/Books: Kelly Vaughn Kramer
Associate Editor: Noah Austin
Creative Director: Barbara Glynn Denney
Art Director: Keith Whitney
Design Production Assistant: Diana Benzel-Rice
Photography Editor: Jeff Kida
Production Director: Michael Bianchi
Production Coordinator: Annette Phares

**WARNING:** Traveling in Arizona, in a wide variety of environments, involves some risk. Weather can be a factor, along with backcountry knowledge. The publisher has attempted to provide accurate information about each drive contained in this book. Users of the guide are urged to obtain information about weather and road conditions from the governing agency that oversees each route prior to undertaking the drives contained herein. The publisher disclaims any liability for injury or other loss or damage incurred while driving any road mentioned in this book.

---

**FRONT COVER:** With the San Francisco Peaks in the background, sunflowers bloom along the loop through Sunset Crater and Wupatki national monuments.
📷 TOM BEAN

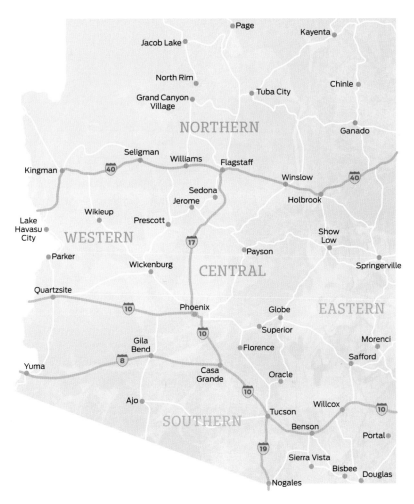

# Contents

52

## NORTHERN ARIZONA

74

## CENTRAL ARIZONA

# Contents

108

130

148

# Using This Guidebook

**E**ach entry in this book includes a narrative about the drive and a map, as well as specific details about mileage, directions, vehicle requirements and where to find more information.

## A. MAPS

The maps in this book are intended as a general reference. For precise road information and routes, please refer to the directions included for each drive, as well as additional sources, such as an *Arizona Atlas & Gazetteer*.

## B. LENGTH

While all mileages in this guide are approximate, this line reveals the distance for each drive, whether a loop, one way or round-trip.

## C. DIRECTIONS

Driving directions are included for each route. Again, mileages are approximate and, in some cases, roads may have more than one designation. Always travel with a map or gazetteer. While we've double-checked these directions, it's good to have a backup.

## D. VEHICLE REQUIREMENTS

In most cases, the roads contained in this guide are accessible to standard vehicles. That said, there are a few instances where a high-clearance vehicle is

required to complete a drive. And, in some cases — *Lava Cave Loop* (page 28), for example — you'll need four-wheel-drive.

## E. INFORMATION

Before you hit the road, it's important to check with your destination's governing agency. In most cases, that's the U.S. Forest Service — we've included phone numbers and websites for specific ranger districts with each entry. Sometimes, road closures, wildfires or acts of nature limit access to a route. Forest rangers will have up-to-date information about what's open where, and they'll be able to answer any questions before you head out the door.

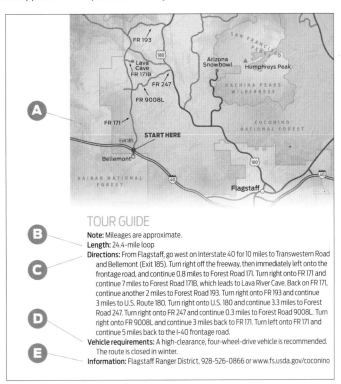

## TOUR GUIDE

**Note:** Mileages are approximate.
**Length:** 24.4-mile loop
**Directions:** From Flagstaff, go west on Interstate 40 for 10 miles to Transwestern Road and Bellemont (Exit 185). Turn right off the freeway, then immediately left onto the frontage road, and continue 0.8 miles to Forest Road 171. Turn right onto FR 171 and continue 7 miles to Forest Road 171B, which leads to Lava River Cave. Back on FR 171, continue another 2 miles to Forest Road 193. Turn right onto FR 193 and continue 3 miles to U.S. Route 180. Turn right onto U.S. 180 and continue 3.3 miles to Forest Road 247. Turn right onto FR 247 and continue 0.3 miles to Forest Road 9008L. Turn right onto FR 9008L and continue 3 miles back to FR 171. Turn left onto FR 171 and continue 5 miles back to the I-40 frontage road.
**Vehicle requirements:** A high-clearance, four-wheel-drive vehicle is recommended. The route is closed in winter.
**Information:** Flagstaff Ranger District, 928-526-0866 or www.fs.usda.gov/coconino

# Introduction

JEFF KIDA

## WHAT TO TAKE

Many of the drives contained in this guide can be completed as day trips, but it's always a good idea to be prepared. While you might want to travel lightly, pack more provisions than you think you'll need, especially when it comes to water.

Basic Equipment
- Map and road atlas or gazetteer
- Water
- Spare tire
- Compass
- Flashlight
- First-aid kit
- Extra food

## SAFETY

Back roads are called back roads for a reason. Nearly all of the drives in this book are just miles from a main thoroughfare, but that doesn't mean you'll always have a cellphone signal or that it would be easy to access help in the event of an emergency. Take these safety factors into consideration:

Flash Floods Flooding is prevalent in Arizona, especially during monsoon season (mid-June through September). Driving in canyons and through washes is especially dangerous during the rainy season, as storms can roll in without warning. So, the warning here is simple: Don't drive through a wash during rainy weather, and never attempt to cross a flooded road in a sedan or any other type of vehicle. Stupid-motorist laws exist for a reason. Don't become a statistic.

Wildlife It's possible to encounter wildlife, from deer and birds to bears, snakes and coyotes, along Arizona's back roads. Should you encounter a wild animal, keep your cool and a safe distance. In addition, proceed slowly — both for the photo opportunity and to avoid a potentially hazardous situation.

## WILDERNESS ETHICS

Leave a place better than you found it. That's the bottom line. It's your job to protect the routes you travel for future generations. Do so by following the seven principles of Leave No Trace.

Plan Ahead and Be Prepared.
- Know the regulations and special concerns for the area you will visit.
- Prepare for extreme weather, hazards and emergencies.
- Schedule your trip to avoid times of high use.
- Visit in small groups when possible.
- Repackage food to minimize waste.

Travel and Camp on Durable Surfaces.
- Durable surfaces include established campsites, rock, gravel, dry grasses or snow.

- Protect riparian areas by camping at least 200 feet from lakes and streams, unless you're in a developed area where specially designated sites are at water's edge.
- Good campsites are found, not made. Altering a site is not necessary.

In popular areas:
- Concentrate use on existing trails and campsites.
- Walk single file in the middle of the trail, even when wet or muddy.
- Keep campsites small. Focus activity in areas where vegetation is absent.

In pristine areas:
- Disperse use to prevent the creation of campsites and trails.
- Avoid places where impacts are just beginning.

### Dispose of Waste Properly.
- Pack it in, pack it out. Inspect your campsite and rest areas for trash or spilled foods. Pack out all trash, leftover food and litter.
- Deposit solid human waste in catholes dug 6 to 8 inches deep, at least 200 feet from water, camp and trails. Cover and disguise the cathole when finished.
- Pack out toilet paper and hygiene products.
- To wash yourself or your dishes, carry water 200 feet away from streams or lakes and use small amounts of biodegradable soap. Scatter strained dishwater.

### Leave What You Find.
- Preserve the past: Examine, but do not touch cultural or historic structures and artifacts.
- Leave rocks, plants and other natural objects as you find them.
- Avoid introducing or transporting non-native species.
- Do not build structures or furniture, and do not dig trenches.

### Minimize Campfire Impacts.
- Campfires can cause lasting impacts to the backcountry. Use a lightweight stove for cooking and enjoy a candle lantern for light.
- Where fires are permitted, use established fire rings, fire pans or mound fires.
- Keep fires small. Only use sticks from the ground that can be broken by hand.
- Burn all wood and coals to ash, put out campfires completely and scatter cool ashes.

### Respect Wildlife.
- Observe wildlife from a distance. Do not follow or approach them.
- Never feed animals. Feeding wildlife damages their health, alters natural behaviors and exposes them to predators and other dangers.
- Protect wildlife and your food by storing rations and trash securely.
- Control pets at all times, or leave them at home.
- Avoid wildlife during sensitive times: mating, nesting, raising young or winter.

### Be Considerate of Other Visitors.
- Respect other visitors and protect the quality of their experience.
- Be courteous. Yield to other users on the trail.
- Step to the downhill side of the trail when encountering pack stock.
- Take breaks and camp away from trails and other visitors.
- Let nature's sounds prevail. Avoid loud voices and noises.

**Source:** *Leave No Trace Center for Outdoor Ethics*

Travelers in Arizona can visit www.az511.gov or dial 511 to get information on road closures, construction, delays, weather and more.

State Route 67, also known as the North Rim Parkway, winds from Jacob Lake to Grand Canyon National Park.

DEREK VON BRIESEN

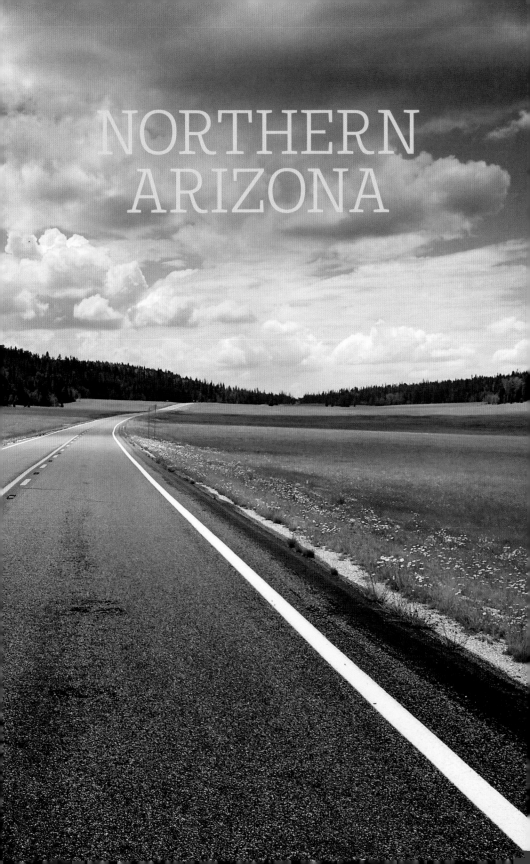

# NORTHERN ARIZONA

# 1

# Bill Williams Mountain Loop

The Bill Williams Mountain Loop makes a short, easy drive through some of the most beautiful ponderosa-pine forest in Northern Arizona, with opportunities to see wildlife and learn a little area history. Beginning in the center of Williams, the drive circles Bill Williams Mountain, which rises to an elevation of 9,170 feet. The 30-mile loop can be completed in an hour or two.

The drive begins at the Williams and Forest Service Visitor Center on Railroad Avenue. The center is located in the historic Atchison, Topeka and Santa Fe Railway freight depot, built in 1901. It's worth a visit. Many of the architectural features remain, as does a freight scale.

Most people think of Williams as a Historic Route 66 town or the southern terminus of the Grand Canyon Railway. The exhibits in the small museum tell the larger story of an area at the center of a

Bill Williams Mountain Loop Road provides striking views of its namesake peak in the distance.
📷 REBECCA WILKS

Sunset colors the clouds above Coleman Lake, an ideal wildlife-watching location.
📷 REBECCA WILKS

well-traveled crossroads, beginning with ancient Indian trade routes. Using these trails, Edward Fitzgerald Beale built his wagon road across the West in the mid-19th century. Portions of that road became Route 66. In between, the Atlantic and Pacific Railroad followed roughly the same course, bringing ranching and timbering.

Of course, the most recent road to follow that well-worn path is Interstate 40. Williams was the last town to have its section of Route 66 bypassed, thanks to lawsuits that kept the last section of I-40 from being built around the town. The suits were dropped after the state agreed to include three exits for Williams. That portion of the interstate opened in 1984, and Route 66 was decommissioned the following year.

From the visitors center, we head west on Railroad Avenue and turn left onto Fourth Street, which becomes Perkinsville Road. Leaving town, we pass the Santa Fe Dam, built in the early 1890s by the railroad. Until the advent of the diesel locomotive, the reservoir created by the dam held water for steam engines traveling through Williams. These days, it's a popular fishing and picnic spot.

After about 6.5 miles, we turn right onto Forest Road 108, the Bill Williams Loop. The wide, well-maintained red-cinder road winds through a lovely stretch of ponderosa-pine forest. Tall, well-spaced pines punctuate a lush carpet of grass, giving way to expansive, high-mountain meadows and occasional rocky outcroppings. The effect is so serene and well-mannered, it looks almost park-like.

After 2 miles, we come to Coleman Lake. Caution signs warn of areas of deep water, but the drought has left the lake looking like little more than marshland. Even so, it's a great place for wildlife-watching. Elk, deer and Merriam's turkeys are common, and bald eagles winter here.

A few miles down the road, a few mule deer run across the road ahead of us. They stop just up the hill to watch us pass. It's likely that we disturbed their visit to MC Tank, a small stock pond at the side of the road that reflects a swimming-pool-blue sky and cotton-ball clouds.

After about 8 miles, we see the turnoff to the Stage Station Trailhead. The 7.9-mile mountain-biking loop winds along a primitive road past a structure that marked a water and rest stop along an old stage route between Williams and Prescott.

Moving on, the forest dips occasionally into juniper grasslands, opening up views of Bill Williams Mountain. After a little more than 18 miles, we hit the pavement and take I-40 back to Williams.

— *Kathy Montgomery*

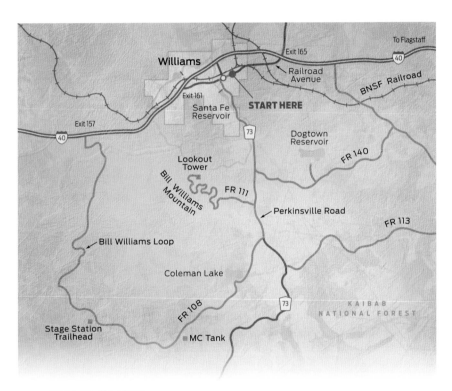

## TOUR GUIDE

**Note:** Mileages are approximate.

**Length:** 30-mile loop

**Directions:** From the Williams Visitor Center (200 W. Railroad Avenue), go west on Railroad Avenue for 0.1 miles to Fourth Street. Turn left onto Fourth Street, which turns into Perkinsville Road (County Road 73), and continue 6.6 miles to Bill Williams Mountain Loop Road (Forest Road 108). Turn right onto Bill Williams Mountain Loop Road and continue 18.3 miles to Interstate 40. Turn right onto I-40 and continue 5 miles back to Williams.

**Vehicle requirements:** None in good weather.

**Information:** Williams Ranger District, 928-635-5600 or www.fs.usda.gov/kaibab

# 2

# Chinle to Cove

The drive to Canyon de Chelly can be deceptive. When you eyeball the route on a map, you can see it's off in the distance, but it doesn't seem *that* far off. That is, until you start driving. Still, it's worth the effort. The long trek to this add-it-to-your-bucket-list-now national monument cuts through the heart of red-rock country on the Navajo Nation, and the scenery is spectacular.

Begin the drive at the Canyon de Chelly Visitor Center, just east of Chinle. From there, head out on Indian Route 64 toward Tsaile and the north rim of Canyon de Chelly. The road skirts the canyon, but unlike the south-rim drive, you won't see much from the road. There are, however, three overlooks that offer great views of Canyon del Muerto's ancient ruins and striking cliff walls.

Royal Arch, near Cove, is a spectacular payoff to a long drive from Chinle.
📷 ROBERT G. McDONALD

Aspens dominate the slopes of the Lukachukai Mountains along the drive from Chinle to Cove.
📷 DAVID MUENCH

Around Mile 21, you'll arrive at the top of a hill where you'll see the Lukachukai and Chuska mountains in the background. Three miles later, you'll reach a "T" junction. This is your cue to turn left onto Indian Route 12.

For the next 8 miles, watch your speed — horses and dogs tend to linger along the road. Although there isn't a sign to indicate that Indian Route 13 will be coming up on your right, the turnoff is at the 32-mile mark of the drive. As you pass through the community of Lukachukai, you'll cross Totsoh Wash, which looks more like a trickle, despite the relatively lush riparian area it feeds. The payoff here is a panorama of red rocks that resemble carved, horizontal waves.

Continuing on IR 13, the road shifts from mostly flat terrain to steep, tight switchbacks. If you're a passenger, your first inclination might be to close your eyes. Don't. Yes, the incline is a little intense, but the views are beautiful. Sagebrush and piñon pines give way to ponderosas and aspens, and at Mile 45, the views of red-rock country get even better.

Eventually, the road starts to descend — minus the winding switchbacks — and arrives at Red Rock Trading Post, which is a good place to fill up or stretch your legs. At this point, you can either turn back and retrace your route or continue on to the remote community of Cove. Surrounded by the Lukachukai and Carrizo mountains, the area is wonderfully scenic, with red-rock formations erupting from the vast, unfolding landscape.

The turnoff to Cove is unmarked, but it's the first left after the trading post on Indian Route 63. From there, make another left onto Indian Route 33. As you meander along, roll down your window and enjoy the views. After 13 miles, the pavement ends, marking the turnaround point. On the way back, the perspective is different, and it's grand. On your left, look for Royal Arch. There's also a nice view of Ship Rock in the distance — across the Arizona-New Mexico border. Although Chinle and Cove are a long way from where you started, you'll be glad you made the trip.

— *Kathy Ritchie*

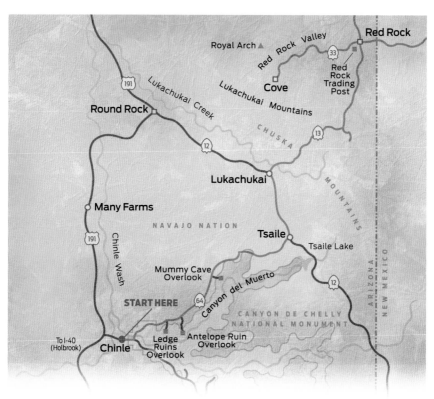

## TOUR GUIDE

**Note:** Mileages are approximate.

**Length:** 70 miles one way

**Directions:** From the Canyon de Chelly Visitor Center, turn right onto Indian Route 64, which veers to the left (follow the sign to Tsaile and the north rim of Canyon de Chelly), and go 24.4 miles to Indian Route 12. Turn left onto IR 12 and continue 8 miles to Indian Route 13. Turn right onto IR 13 and continue 24.5 miles to Indian Route 63. Turn left onto IR 63 and continue 0.5 miles to Indian Route 33. Turn left onto IR 33 and continue 13 miles to the turnaround point.

**Vehicle requirements:** The route is suitable for standard sedans, but traveling in inclement weather requires a four-wheel-drive.

**Information:** Canyon de Chelly National Monument, 928-674-5500 or www.nps.gov/cach

# 3

# Hart Prairie

**A**spens are the essence of fall in Arizona. If you're not of that opinion, you might change your mind after driving along Hart Prairie Road (Forest Road 151). This 10-mile scenic stretch is an easy addition to a day in Flagstaff or a worthwhile diversion on the way to the Grand Canyon. The journey into golden splendor begins approximately 10 miles north of town, just off U.S. Route 180.

A medley of yellow-tipped common mullein, purple thistles and lavender asters offers the first splashes of color beneath an awning of ponderosa pines. As the dirt road crests the hill after 1 mile, you won't miss the first glimpse of aspens, neon beacons shining through a sea of pines on the right. These saplings herald a small taste of the treasures to come.

Add a half-mile along a road that curves like a river, and the pines part to reveal open skies and meadows accented by the San Francisco Peaks. When the Grateful Dead wrote *Fire on the Mountain*, the band's inspiration could have been Humphreys Peak. With bright plumes of aspens flanking its sides, the mountain appears swathed in a vibrant flame.

Hart Prairie Road, which features great views of the San Francisco Peaks, has an idyllic feel.
📷 TOM BEAN

The San Francisco Peaks rise above fall-colored aspen trees. The peaks are sacred to several Native American tribes.

📷 TOM BEAN

Intimate views — close enough to see carvings of names and hearts marring the trees' white bark — first appear around 3 miles. The air might be chilly, but it's worth rolling your window down to view autumn's brilliant colors, as orange leaves mingle with green grasses and auburn ferns. Pass over a cattle guard, and clumps of aspens dominate fields to the left as the road reaches a plateau.

When the scenery morphs into meadows, look for songbirds like swallows and flycatchers near Hart Prairie Preserve, a former homestead. From 1892 to 1901, stagecoaches taking visitors from Flagstaff to the South Rim stopped here for rest and refreshments. Now, herds of elk and deer frequent the area. The Nature Conservancy offers guided tours of the preserve until early October.

Barbed wire and wooden fences farther along mark private property; be alert to runners, walkers and ATV riders sharing the occasionally rutted and rocky road. At 6 miles, FR 151 intersects Bismarck Lake Road (Forest Road 627). For those wanting to hike, this detour leads to a trailhead in the Kachina Peaks Wilderness.

Nature showcases her own magical version of the yellow brick road as aspen leaves line the way forward. More still swirl downward at the slightest breeze and create a melody of soft bells. Those that don't reach the ground cling like ornaments to the needles of subalpine firs. Wait to pull over and make pictures when the road widens to fit two cars at 7 miles.

The steadily descending drive passes an idyllic log cabin just before intersecting Forest Road 418. Stay left and follow the signs for U.S. 180, noting the dark-red shade the road imbues as it trades a tunnel of aspen for fire-scarred land.

Ghostly spires of charred pines are jagged tombstones giving way to aspens, early successional species that thrive after natural disturbances. Glide smoothly along gently rolling roads as you bid farewell to the last sprinklings of fall foliage.

— *Leah Duran*

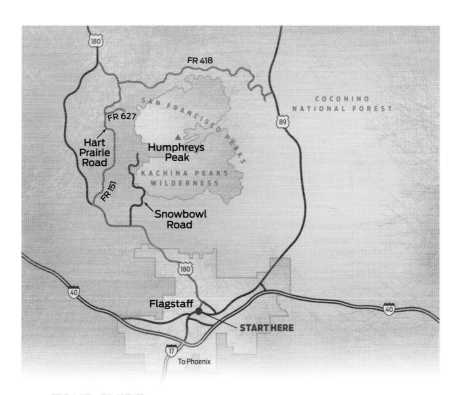

## TOUR GUIDE

**Note:** Mileages are approximate.

**Length:** 10 miles one way

**Directions:** From Flagstaff, go northwest on U.S. Route 180 for 10 miles to Forest Road 151 (Hart Prairie Road). Turn right onto Hart Prairie Road and continue 8 miles to an intersection with Forest Road 418. Veer left to stay on FR 151, then continue 2 miles to U.S. 180.

**Vehicle requirements:** Although the dirt road is rutted and rocky in some places, it is accessible to all vehicles. As with most back roads, however, a high-clearance vehicle is recommended.

**Information:** Flagstaff Ranger District, 928-526-0866 or www.fs.usda.gov/coconino

# 4

# Indian Road 6910

When it comes to waterfalls in Arizona, the first thought for most people is Havasu Falls, and rightfully so. However, the Colorado River is fed by another watery wonder: Grand Falls. Although it's a lesser-known kid sister, Grand Falls is more accessible than Havasu, and it's about the last thing you'd expect to encounter in the arid expanse of Ňavajoland.

"Mud Falls," as Grand Falls is sometimes called, is fed exclusively by snow-melt and rainfall, so it often runs low or doesn't run at all. The falls, though they look like something created by Willy Wonka, were formed when lava from a nearby crater created a dam in the Little Colorado River and rerouted the flow. The falls are where the new route rejoins the

A monsoon storm produces heavy rain along Leupp Road on the Navajo Nation.
📷 MIKE OLBINSKI

After rain or sufficient snowmelt, Grand Falls lives up to its other name: "Chocolate Falls."
📷 SHANE McDERMOTT

old one. After a rainy spring or late-summer monsoon storms, enough water usually passes through the falls' red-dirt path to create a muddy cascade. In the wake of a wet winter, the 185-foot drop can resemble a chocolate Niagara Falls, making it aesthetically delicious and worth the grating drive.

The first 37.4 miles from Flagstaff are comfortably paved — first eastbound along Interstate 40, then north along Winona and Leupp roads, where you'll catch glimpses of the area's cinder mines. These shaved volcanic cones reveal layers of ages-old burgundy, black and caramel rocks.

After passing through the little town of Winona, Leupp Road (where keen mileage calculation should begin) leads to the Navajo Nation. There, the signs of human life are pleasantly fewer, while signs of the area's unique geological history abound. The road bends past untouched cinder cones and craters that tower up from an otherwise even landscape, interrupting distant views of the San Francisco Peaks.

About 17 miles from the start of Leupp Road, signs for the Grand Falls Bible Church start to appear. The church and the falls are on different roads and are many miles apart, but it's a good time to pay close attention to the odometer and mileposts. Indian Road 6910 materializes approximately 20.3 miles down Leupp Road, between mileposts 5 and 6. There's a small official sign, but it's hard to see in advance.

After taking a left onto the unpaved road, there's a sprinkling of small hills and rock outcroppings, but, for the most part, the land is dry and flat as far as the eye can see. You'll struggle with the idea that any semblance of water exists anywhere along this road. Another struggle is the steering wheel. Although IR

6910 looks smooth, it's painfully graded and can be dangerous at high speeds. Fortunately, the need to soak up the solitude and beauty of Navajoland will trump the need for speed.

After 9.4 miles, and after passing Indian Road 70, several side-by-side dirt roads veer off to the left. Picnic-table ramadas and the likely existence of other vehicles are clues that something is out there, but it's still hard to imagine. Only after you've parked your car and walked the short distance to the overlook will you believe that Grand Falls actually exists. But there it is — very different from Havasu Falls, but impressive nonetheless.

— *JoBeth Jamison*

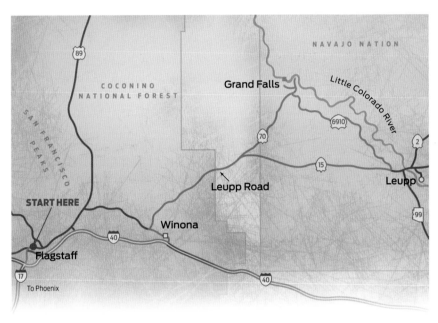

## TOUR GUIDE

**Note:** Mileages are approximate.

**Length:** 47 miles one way

**Directions:** From Flagstaff, go east on Interstate 40 for 15 miles to Winona Road (Exit 211). Turn left (north) onto Winona Road and continue 2.1 miles to Leupp Road. Turn right onto Leupp Road and continue 20.3 miles to Indian Road 6910 (unmarked). Turn left onto IR 6910 and continue 9.4 miles to an unmarked road. Turn left onto the unmarked road and continue 0.2 miles to the Grand Falls overlook.

**Vehicle requirements:** A high-clearance, four-wheel-drive vehicle is required. The road is graded but very rough and slow-going. Snow, ice, deep water and mud may be present.

**Travel advisory:** Grand Falls is located on the Navajo Nation, where it's illegal to travel off designated roads. Proceed respectfully. There are no barriers or fences, so keep dogs leashed and children in hand.

**Information:** Navajo Division of Transportation, 505-371-8300 or www.navajodot.org

# 5

# Lava Cave Loop

In the heat of summer, there's no better place to take a road trip than Flagstaff, and no better route than this 24.4-mile loop, which winds along shady forest roads past wildflower-filled meadows and includes a short detour to Lava River Cave, Northern Arizona's natural icebox.

We begin at Forest Road 171, about 10 miles west of Flagstaff. The gravel road is bumpy but wide and straight as it runs through a well-managed ponderosa-pine forest, which occasionally gives way to wide, grassy meadows strewn with volcanic rock.

After a few miles, the road opens to views of Kendrick Peak, one of the larger volcanoes in the San Francisco Volcanic Field. Rising to an elevation of more than 10,000 feet, it's an impressive sight.

After 7 miles, we turn right onto Forest Road 171B and drive the quarter-mile to the parking area for Lava River Cave. The entrance to the cave is located about 300 yards east of the parking area, marked by a circle of rocks and a plaque.

The lava-tube cave is three-quarters of a mile long, the longest of its kind in Arizona. Geologists believe it formed in a matter of hours about 700,000 years ago, when lava erupted from a nearby volcanic vent. The tube formed as the top and sides cooled, but the molten river continued to flow through the center.

Because it formed quickly, the cave floor is like a river frozen in time, with ripples and the rocks the lava was carrying suspended in place. The ceiling drips with "lavacicles," which formed as hot gas shot through the cave shortly after it formed, partially re-melting the lava.

Lumbermen discovered the cave around 1915. Because the temperature inside remains in the 30s and 40s

Forest Road 171 runs through ponderosa pines and grassy meadows near Lava River Cave.
📷 JEFF KIDA

The gravel Forest Road 171 winds into a ponderosa forest.
📷 JEFF KIDA

year-round, homesteaders once collected ice from the cave to use for refrigeration.

The tube is slippery, jagged in places and very dark. The U.S. Forest Service advises bringing three light sources in case one fails. Headlamps are recommended to keep hands free. The hike is 1.5 miles in and back, and it ranges from a wide, spacious tunnel to a short crab crawl.

Back on FR 171, we could continue straight for another 4 miles to the trailhead for Kendrick Peak. Instead, we turn right after 2 miles onto Forest Road 193. On this road, we catch occasional glimpses of the San Francisco Peaks and see a small grove of aspens, the first of our drive, growing out of a rocky outcrop.

After 3 miles, we pick up U.S. Route 180, turn right and continue south. This stretch is scattered with stands of aspen, their small leaves glittering like the sequins of a party dress against paper-white legs.

After another 3.3 miles, we turn right onto Forest Road 247. It's easy to miss, but we find the turnoff just north of Milepost 229, about a mile south of the well-marked turnoff for Forest Road 245.

After a quarter-mile, we turn right onto Forest Road 9008L, a logging road, and creep slowly along the rocky, rutted road, which is not much wider than a hiking trail. Here, the forest feels intimate. It crowds the road, which is littered with pine needles and almost completely shaded. An Abert's squirrel, with its long, tasseled ears, runs across the road ahead of us.

After 3 miles, we emerge again onto FR 171, turn left and drive the 5 miles back to where we started, with just enough time to head back to Flagstaff for a late lunch.

— *Kathy Montgomery*

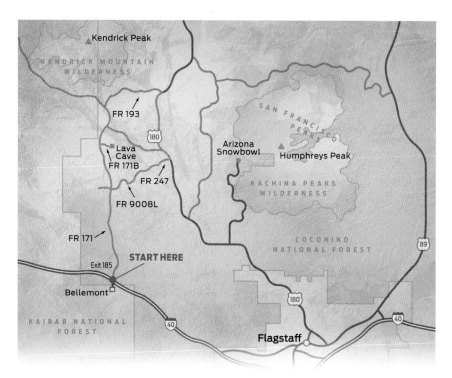

## TOUR GUIDE

**Note:** Mileages are approximate.

**Length:** 24.4-mile loop

**Directions:** From Flagstaff, go west on Interstate 40 for 10 miles to Transwestern Road and Bellemont (Exit 185). Turn right off the freeway, then immediately left onto the frontage road, and continue 0.8 miles to Forest Road 171. Turn right onto FR 171 and continue 7 miles to Forest Road 171B, which leads to Lava River Cave. Back on FR 171, continue another 2 miles to Forest Road 193. Turn right onto FR 193 and continue 3 miles to U.S. Route 180. Turn right onto U.S. 180 and continue 3.3 miles to Forest Road 247. Turn right onto FR 247 and continue 0.3 miles to Forest Road 9008L. Turn right onto FR 9008L and continue 3 miles back to FR 171. Turn left onto FR 171 and continue 5 miles back to the I-40 frontage road.

**Vehicle requirements:** A high-clearance, four-wheel-drive vehicle is recommended. The route is closed in winter.

**Information:** Flagstaff Ranger District, 928-526-0866 or www.fs.usda.gov/coconino

# 6

# North Rim Parkway

If you're wondering where Mother Nature spends her summers, this is it. The Grand Canyon, the vast meadows, the evergreens and aspens, the cool breezes, the quiet ... there's nothing quite like the Kaibab Plateau and its 44-mile parkway, which begins at Jacob Lake.

Named for Jacob Hamblin, a Mormon pioneer known as the "Buckskin Apostle," Jacob Lake is home to the oldest existing ranger station in the United States. It's also home to the Jacob Lake Inn, a small place that's big on making cookies. The chocolate-chip and peanut-butter cookies are as good as any cookies anywhere, but if you're up for something different, try the lemon-zucchini. Cookies are a must, and so is a visit to the Kaibab Plateau Visitor Center. It's located next door to the inn, and it offers information on the surrounding national forest, Marble Canyon, the Kanab Creek and Saddle Mountain wilderness areas, camping, hiking, pine cones and just about anything else you'll need to know. It's also a good place to stock up on maps and Smokey the Bear logo wear. Buy a T-shirt. It'll be a good reminder that only you can prevent forest fires.

Although this drive technically begins at Jacob Lake, the approach to that point is pretty impressive, too. From Flagstaff, the route winds north over the Navajo Nation, crosses the Colorado River south of Page, parallels the spectacular

---

Multicolored wildflowers sprout from a tree-lined meadow on the North Rim of Grand Canyon National Park.
📷 JACK DYKINGA

Fog shrouds evergreens at DeMotte Park along the North Rim Parkway.
📷 TOM BEAN

Vermilion Cliffs and eventually climbs into the pines at Jacob Lake.

From there, the road heads south for a few miles through a gorgeous stand of ponderosa pines and quaking aspens. There's something comforting about a drive in the trees. Whatever it is, you'll get that feeling along this stretch. The parkway, by the way, follows an old livestock trail that was used by Mormon settlers and early visitors to the Canyon, some of whom carved their initials into the defenseless aspens.

About the time you've finished your first lemon-zucchini cookie, you'll see the remains of the Warm Fire, which was started by a lightning strike on June 8, 2006. In all, it burned nearly 60,000 acres between Jacob Lake and Demotte Park. Despite the loss of life, a new generation of aspens is quickly taking over. It helps mitigate the damage.

Moving on, the plateau gradually rises to a point where Douglas firs and white firs take over. The dense mixed-conifer forest is an ideal place to spot wildlife. Be on the lookout for mule deer, wild turkeys, chukars, coyotes, Kaibab squirrels and maybe even a California condor. Animals, animals, animals ... Teddy Roosevelt was so impressed with the nature of things around here that he officially named it the Grand Canyon Game Preserve in 1906. This might even be where he picked up his big stick.

Heading south, the forest changes once again near Crane Lake. Here, Engelmann spruce and subalpine firs rule the roost. Perhaps even more enjoyable, though, are the large grassy meadows. If you haven't made any photos up to this point, get your camera ready. This is where the deer and the antelope play — so to speak. Also, if you have the time, head off on one of the adjacent forest roads. They make spectacular side trips, and some of them will take you all the way to the various rims of the Canyon (see *North Rim Viewpoints*, page 36).

Back on the parkway, near the border of the Kaibab National Forest and Grand Canyon National Park, you'll come to the remains of another fire. The damage from the Outlet Fire is less evident than what you'll have seen back at the Warm Fire site, but it's enough to make you glad you bought that Smokey T-shirt.

From there, you'll eventually arrive at the North Rim of the national park, which features some great hikes, picnic areas, the Grand Canyon Lodge and, of course, one of the seven natural wonders of the world. No wonder Mother Nature spends her summers here.

— *Robert Stieve*

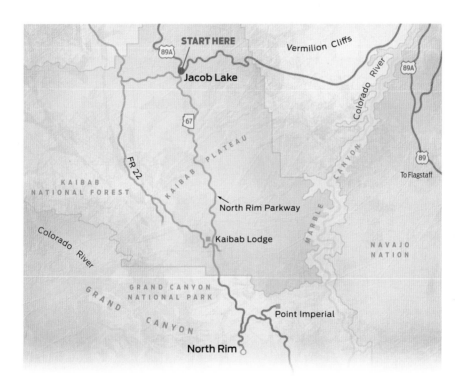

## TOUR GUIDE

**Note:** Mileages are approximate.

**Length:** 30 miles one way (to the park entrance)

**Directions:** From Flagstaff, go north on U.S. Route 89 for 110 miles to U.S. Route 89A (25 miles south of Page). Turn left onto U.S. 89A and continue 55 miles to Jacob Lake. The scenic drive starts on State Route 67 at Jacob Lake and continues for 30 miles to the entrance of Grand Canyon National Park. The rim itself is 14 miles farther south.

**Vehicle requirements:** None

**Information:** North Kaibab Ranger District, 928-643-7395 or www.fs.usda.gov/kaibab

# 7

# North Rim
# Viewpoints

There's a thought that crosses the mind of almost every first-time visitor to the Grand Canyon: *Imagine being the explorer who discovered this natural wonder. One minute you're riding a horse across the high desert, and then, suddenly ... WHOA! How incredible it must have been to stand alone on the rim, with no previous knowledge of the Canyon's existence.*

Today, with 4.5 million people a year descending on the national park, that kind of solitude is hard to find. It's not impossible, though. You just have to know where to go, and that's where this drive comes in.

Naturally, if you're willing to hoof it, there are hundreds, even thousands, of places where you can find some peace and quiet in the Grand Canyon, but to find one that's reachable by car is a little more challenging. Timp Point is one of the few. It's isolated, to be sure, and it's also scenic — the panoramas

North Timp Point offers a stunning panorama of the Grand Canyon, including Steamboat Mountain.
📷 SHANE MCDERMOTT

Ponderosa pines and aspens line one of the many forest roads on the Grand Canyon's North Rim.

📷 DEREK VON BRIESEN

from the point are unlike any you've ever seen of the Grand Canyon. Although Timp Point is the payoff, the drive out there and some of the side trips are pretty spectacular, too.

The route begins at Jacob Lake, which, at an elevation of more than 7,900 feet, is a cool and idyllic place to pitch a tent or rent a room. It's also the home of the Kaibab Plateau Visitor Center. You'll want to stop in, stock up on maps and get the lay of the land.

From there, follow State Route 67 — one of the most scenic drives in Arizona (see *North Rim Parkway*, page 32) — south for 27.5 miles through postcard landscapes of ponderosa pines, aspens, spruce and broad green meadows to Forest Road 22. Turn right onto FR 22 and start looking for wildlife. Within a minute, FR 22 cuts into the woods, and the trees stick around for the next 10.5 miles to Forest Road 206. At the junction, turn left onto FR 206 and continue south for 3.5 miles to Forest Road 214. There, you can either make a side trip out to Parissawampitts Point, from which you can see Tapeats Amphitheater and Fishtail Mesa, or continue south toward Timp Point. It's a 16-mile round-trip detour to Parissawampitts, but it's well worth the effort. Either way, from the intersection of FR 206 and FR 214, continue south on FR 206 for a little more than a mile to Forest Road 271.

The countryside along all of these easy-to-follow dirt roads is classic Kaibab National Forest: lush evergreens, aspens, summer grasses and wildflowers. The fauna is impressive, too. In addition to deer, turkeys and mountain lions, keep your eyes peeled for Kaibab squirrels, which are shy, dark animals with tufted ears and bushy white tails.

Moving along, turn right onto FR 271 and drive for about 5 miles to a junction with Forest Road 271A, which leads to North Timp Point, another worthy diversion that offers views (with binoculars) of Thunder River, a large spring that gushes from an opening in the north wall of Tapeats Canyon. To get to Timp Point, stay left on FR 271 and continue for another 3 miles. This is the end of the road — the quiet place with the booming payoff.

Along with the 270-degree panoramas of one of the worlds's seven natural wonders, you'll also see Steamboat Mountain rising up from the Canyon floor.

What you won't see are people, which makes Timp Point an ideal place to imagine what it was like to discover the Grand Canyon.

Enjoy the views, and plan on staying awhile. There's nothing like standing alone on an isolated Canyon rim. It's a sensation that will stay with you as you retrace your steps back to Jacob Lake.

— *Robert Stieve*

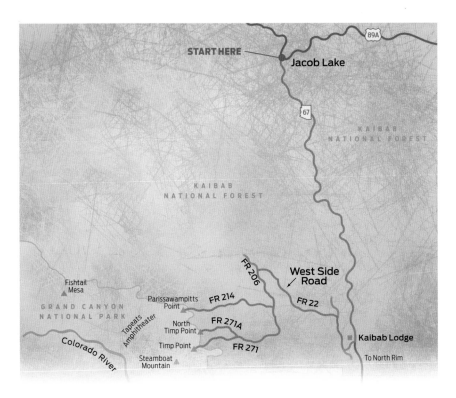

## TOUR GUIDE

**Note:** Mileages are approximate.

**Length:** 73 miles one way (Jacob Lake to Timp Point, including side trips to Parissawampitts Point and North Timp Point)

**Directions:** From Jacob Lake, go south on State Route 67 for 27.5 miles to Forest Road 22. Turn right onto FR 22 and continue 10.5 miles to a "Y" junction with Forest Road 206. Turn left onto FR 206 and continue 3.5 miles to Forest Road 214. After a 16-mile (round-trip) detour on FR 214 to Parissawampitts Point, continue on FR 206 for 1.5 miles to Forest Road 271. Turn right onto FR 271 and continue 5 miles to Forest Road 271A. After a 6-mile (round-trip) detour on FR 271A to North Timp Point, continue on FR 271 for 3 miles to Timp Point.

**Vehicle requirements:** Unless rain or snow is present, this route is accessible to all vehicles. SR 67 closes during the winter; call the North Kaibab Ranger District office before your trip to determine whether the route is open.

**Information:** North Kaibab Ranger District, 928-643-7395 or www.fs.usda.gov/kaibab

· 8

# Point Sublime

**W**hen the payoff on a scenic drive is something called Point Sublime, it's reasonable to think that the drive itself might fall short. In this case, it doesn't. Not even close. The old-growth ponderosas are part of that. So are the other evergreens, the wildflowers, the meadows and the extreme solitude that'll make you wonder: *Why aren't there more cars lined up? Sublime ... that means stupendous, right? Why am I the only one out here?* You'll be intrigued by the isolation, but not for long. You'll be too busy looking around.

The drive begins a couple miles north of the North Rim's Grand Canyon Lodge. From the park road, look for a sign on the left that marks the Widforss Trail. Although the focus here is the ride out to Point Sublime, Widforss is worth remembering — it's one of the best trails in Arizona. Just past the trailhead, the dirt road veers right and slips into the forest. A few hundred yards later, it splits. Veer left and follow the signs. You'll see a lot of lupines at the outset, and at the 1.5-mile mark, an elderly ponderosa surrounded by youthful aspens.

"Your way is lined with heavy growth of the Kaibab Forest," longtime editor Raymond Carlson wrote in the September 1941 issue of *Arizona Highways*.

The view from the Grand Canyon's Point Sublime is worthy of the long drive required to reach it.
📷 JACK DYKINGA

Lupines crowd the roadside along the narrow, rough route to Point Sublime.
📷 GARY LADD

"Pine trees cluster about your path, shouldering each other to get a better look at you. You come across small meadows, where a deer will look up, almost annoyed by the intrusion. Flowers carpet the forest, having a high old time in the sunlight."

The trees still cluster, especially in the early stages, where the road narrows to a single lane. Then, about 4 miles in, the road widens a bit and crests a hill. Up ahead you'll see the drive's most impressive meadow. The road slices through the middle of it for a mile and a half and then dips back into the woods. Bright-green ferns and deep-orange ponderosas mark the passage. A couple of miles later, you'll go through a small burn area and another meadow, and then re-enter the woods, where the first tree is a hulking ponderosa. Although the forest on the Kaibab Plateau is blessed with quaking aspens, Engelmann spruce and Douglas firs, it's the ponderosas that stand out most.

Just beyond the old yellow belly, the road heads up a steep, rocky hillside. You'll need a high-clearance vehicle — four-wheel-drive if you have it. The rest of the road is in pretty good shape, weather permitting, as it weaves through the thick, alpine forest. A few miles beyond the rough spot, you'll come to an intersection. The short detour to the left is the first good opportunity to see the Canyon — in case you forgot, there is a natural wonder over there. To get to Point Sublime, go the other way, and within a few minutes, you'll come to another intersection. To the right is Fire Point, but you'll veer left.

Other than those two side roads and a smattering of sawed-off trees, there are no signs of man on the road to Point Sublime. Enjoy the scenic beauty and pay attention to your odometer. At the 12.1-mile mark, you'll get a glimpse of the Canyon to the left, but it's just a glimpse. A half-mile later, the views make another appearance before the road winds back into the woods.

Things remain about the same for the next 4 miles. That's when you'll start to sense the abyss off to your right. Moments later, *bam*, there it is. The Grand Canyon. Despite your natural inclination to stare at Mother Nature's handiwork, keep your eyes on the road. There are sheer drop-offs to your right, and a half-mile later, the drop-offs close in on both sides of the road.

Take a deep breath and make the short but harrowing ride out to the point. "Out there," Mr. Carlson wrote in 1941, "is a view of the Grand Canyon you'll see from no other place but Point Sublime." Sublime is certainly one of the words that'll come to mind. Stunning, spectacular, sensational ... those will occur to you, too. It's a payoff that's worthy of the drive that takes you to it.

— *Robert Stieve*

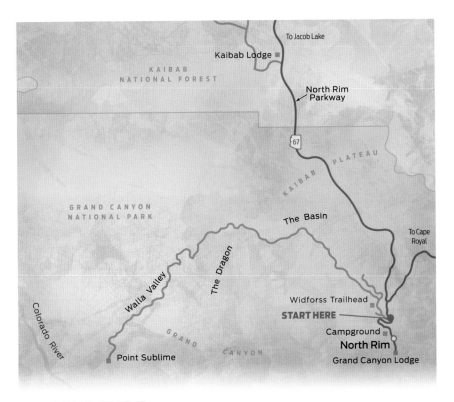

## TOUR GUIDE

**Note:** Mileages are approximate.

**Length:** 17.7 miles one way

**Directions:** From Grand Canyon Lodge on the North Rim, go north on the park road for 2.6 miles to the turnoff for the Widforss Trail. Turn left and continue 17.7 miles to Point Sublime.

**Vehicle requirements:** A high-clearance vehicle is required; four-wheel-drive is recommended.

**Information:** Grand Canyon National Park, 928-638-7888 or www.nps.gov/grca

## 9

# Stoneman Lake Road

**F**or people on a mission, the surest route to Flagstaff from Phoenix is a straight shot up Interstate 17. It's quick, and it's scenic in its own right, especially as it runs into the cool ponderosa-pine forest. But travelers looking for a quieter route will find Stoneman Lake Road (Forest Road 213) the perfect byway to connect to Forest Highway 3, a back road into Flagstaff.

The 14-mile trip begins off I-17, some 19 miles north of Camp Verde at Exit 306, and takes about 40 minutes. There are, however, plenty of opportunities to stop and enjoy the scenery, which might lead to a longer excursion. The first 6 miles are paved, and although the last 8 traverse a rustic road, it's well maintained and easily passable in a standard passenger vehicle, but not after heavy rains.

As the juniper-lined paved road ends, you'll bear left and continue on FR 213 — onto a red dirt road — and begin a slow, steady climb. After approximately 2 miles, the road splits to the day-use area for Stoneman Lake. The road to the lake comprises several semi-hairy turns, but the few seconds of adrenaline amplification are worth it. At the end of the road, bear right into the public parking lot.

Created more than 8 million years ago by a volcanic depression, the lake is a closed system, meaning there's no outflow to remove pollutants. That, however, hasn't stopped a veritable

Stoneman Lake Road isn't all paved, but it's well maintained and passable in a sedan in good weather.
📷 LYNN SANKEY

A gnarled juniper overlooks Stoneman Lake, where you'll find boating opportunities and picnic areas.
📷 NICK BEREZENKO

menagerie of wildlife from flocking to the area. Among the fish that inhabit the lake are yellow perch and northern pike. In addition, countless songbirds nest in the area, and on any given day, you might catch the blue-winged flash of a Steller's jay out of the corner of your eye. Bald eagles are also fond of the lake and its surrounding trees and basalt boulders — during winter, the area becomes a nesting ground for the national bird.

Boats with a single electric motor are allowed on the lake and can launch from a public gravel boat landing. If you're more interested in a leisurely picnic before hitting the road to Flagstaff, make use of one of the shaded picnic tables or pick a pretty place on the lakeshore. Take care, though, not to disturb any of the private cottages that line the lake.

After you explore Stoneman Lake, return to FR 213 and continue on as the road rambles in and out of private land and through pine and aspen forests and a speckling of wide-open meadows and public campgrounds. After another 6 miles, you'll reach a junction with Forest Road 230, which ultimately leads to the base of Apache Maid Mountain, looming more than 7,000 feet over Wet Beaver Creek. That route loops back to Stoneman Lake Road. Or you can bypass the scenic drive to Apache Maid Mountain and continue directly to FH 3, which is yet another scenic drive that leads to Flagstaff.

— *Kelly Vaughn Kramer*

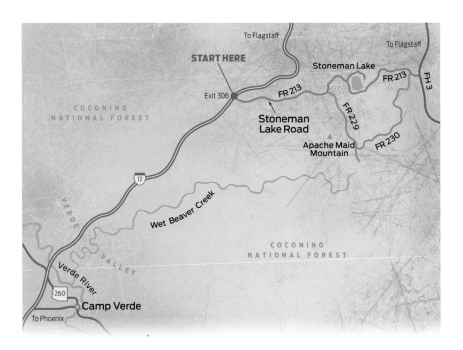

## TOUR GUIDE

**Note:** Mileages are approximate.

**Distance:** 14 miles one way (to Lake Mary Road)

**Directions:** From Phoenix, go north on Interstate 17 for 106 miles to Stoneman Lake Road (Exit 306). Turn right onto Stoneman Lake Road (Forest Road 213) and continue 6 miles until the pavement ends. Bear left to stay on FR 213, then continue 2 miles to the Stoneman Lake day-use area or 8 miles to Lake Mary Road (Forest Highway 3).

**Vehicle requirements:** None in good weather, but four-wheel-drive is recommended in rain or snow.

**Information:** Red Rock Ranger District, 928-203-2900 or www.fs.usda.gov/coconino

# 10

# Sycamore Canyon Vista

Sycamore Canyon is Arizona's second-largest gorge — second only to the natural wonder that can be seen from outer space. The attributes of the Grand Canyon are many, but the state's runner-up has a few of its own, including the 13-mile drive to reach it. It's a picturesque route through the Kaibab National Forest that gets less traffic than a Sonoran Desert highway in the dead of summer.

The drive begins on Garland Prairie Road, which intersects with Interstate 40 just east of Williams. After crossing a set of train tracks, stay left until you merge onto a well-maintained dirt road and head into the first of several thick stands of ponderosa pines.

A few miles in, you'll come to another fork. Turn

Garland Prairie, along the route to Sycamore Canyon Vista, offers an unobstructed view of the San Francisco Peaks to the northeast.
📷 TOM BEAN

A hedgehog cactus blooms at Sycamore Canyon Vista, the payoff to a quarter-mile hike from Forest Road 56.
📷 TOM BEAN

left and continue to McDougal Flat, a large clearing that offers a nice view of the San Francisco Peaks on the left. From there, it's back into the ponderosas, where you'll see signs directing you toward the Sycamore Canyon Vista Trailhead.

Following the signs, you'll end up on Forest Road 56, another good dirt road. It narrows to one lane in places and gets a little rough in others. Mind your speed, roll down the windows and enjoy the sights and sounds of the high country. At Mile 11, you'll come to a turnoff that leads to the Sycamore Rim Trail, but that's a hike for another day. Keep going straight until FR 56 dead-ends at the trailhead.

A map of the canyon's entire trail system is posted there. Many of the hikes are long, but the trail to Sycamore Canyon Vista is only a quarter-mile. From the viewpoint, you'll get a good look at Arizona's second-largest canyon, as well as a glimpse of Sycamore Creek on the canyon floor.

Because the 21-mile-long canyon is a protected wilderness area, there aren't any roads or campgrounds within it — just the canyon's namesake sycamores, along with ponderosas and other evergreens. If you move quietly, you might see deer or elk at the vista, as well as lizards and birds. Enjoy the view. It's not the Grand Canyon, but, as you'll see, that won't matter.

— *Noah Austin*

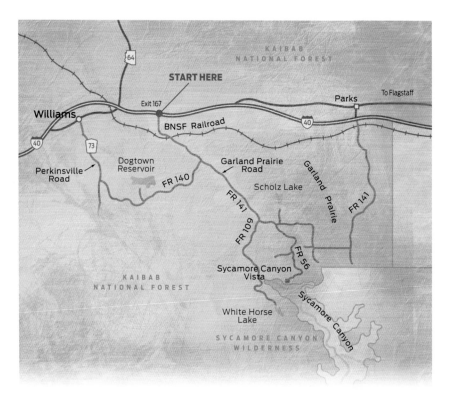

## TOUR GUIDE

**Note:** Mileages are approximate.

**Length:** 13 miles one way

**Directions:** From Flagstaff, go west on Interstate 40 for 28 miles to Exit 167 (Garland Prairie Road). Turn left onto Garland Prairie Road, which later becomes Forest Road 141, and continue 9 miles to Forest Road 56. Turn right onto FR 56 and continue 4 miles to the Sycamore Canyon Vista trailhead.

**Vehicle requirements:** None; however, a high-clearance vehicle is recommended in inclement weather.

**Information:** Williams Ranger District, 928-635-5600 or www.fs.usda.gov/kaibab

# 11

# Volcanoes & Ruins Loop

**P**ick up a course catalog for Northern Arizona University, and you'll find the usual list of electives: history, geology, archaeology. It's not rocket science, but if you want to learn about yesteryear, volcanoes and artifacts, NAU is a great place to start.

Another option is a Sunday drive through Sunset Crater Volcano and Wupatki national monuments. History, geology and archaeology, as well as many other "ologies," are part of the education you'll get on this 73-mile scenic loop. Of course, if you'd rather just sit back and enjoy the ride, you can do that, too.

The paved loop begins near Bonito Park Campground, which sits in the shadow of Sunset Crater. Before you take off, take a look around. Virtually every mountain you'll see is volcanic — in all, there are 600 volcanoes in the area. Sunset Crater is the youngest, and like its many siblings, it's dormant. In A.D. 1040, however, it blew its top. The eruptions continued, on and off, for almost 200 years, eventually creating the 1,000-foot cinder cone we see today.

The Navajo call it "Yellow-Topped Mountain"; the Hopi call it "Red Hill." In 1885, Colorado River explorer John Wesley Powell penned his own description: "A portion of the cone is of bright reddish cinders, while the adjacent rocks are of black basalt. The contrast in the colors is so great that on viewing the mountain from a distance the red cinders seem to be on fire. From this circumstance, the cone has been named Sunset Peak ... which seems to glow with a light of its own."

Regardless of its renown, the Northern Arizona landmark was almost destroyed in 1928 when a movie production company wanting to film a landslide proposed blowing up the crater. Fortunately, the locals weren't crazy about the idea, and pushed for the crater's protection, which it received on May 26, 1930, when President Herbert Hoover established Sunset Crater National Monument. The word "Volcano" was added to the name in 1990, and today, the park comprises 3,040 acres

Wukoki Pueblo is one of the largest surviving pueblos at Wupatki National Monument.
📷 GEORGE STOCKING

Sunset Crater Volcano erupted intermittently for almost 200 years, creating the cinder cone it is today.
📷 TOM BROWNOLD

surrounded by the Coconino National Forest.

The crater itself is the main attraction in the monument, and one of the best ways to see it is by hiking the road that meanders up O'Leary Peak — the turnoff is just before the visitors center. A few miles farther is the Bonito Lava Flow. If you've never been to the moon, this is what it looks like. In fact, it's so lunar-like, NASA had its Apollo astronauts (including Neil Armstrong) train here in the 1960s.

There's a short trail you can take to experience the rocks — you'll feel like you're climbing around in Mother Nature's barbecue grill. Near the base of the crater, another trail passes squeeze-ups, fumaroles and clinkers (volcanic terms worth learning about in person).

Heading north from the higher elevations near Sunset Crater Volcano National Monument to the desert grasslands of Wupatki National Monument, you'll eventually come upon the abandoned ruins of the Sinagua people.

The Sinaguans (our name, not theirs) were farmers who were forced north by Sunset Crater's eruption and learned to use the dark ash as a kind of mulch, which conserved the area's scarce moisture longer than the native soil. Modern science would later demonstrate that cinder ash also aids in corn germination and growth. Drought eventually forced the Sinaguans out, but in their wake, they left behind a series of magnificent structures — most of their stone homes are so well preserved that even present-day visitors think they've been restored. They're not.

To date, archaeologists have mapped and studied more than 2,500 sites within Wupatki National Monument. The largest of these pueblos — Wukoki, Lomaki and Wupatki — are open to the public. In its heyday, Wupatki contained more than 100 rooms, and things stayed mostly intact until the 1880s, when sheepherders used the ruins as a camp. Although looters eventually cleaned them out, they're definitely worth a look.

From the ruins, the rest of the loop winds for about 10 miles back to U.S. Route 89. It's a peaceful drive, and with all the history, geology and archaeology out of the way, it's the perfect time to sit back and enjoy the ride.

— *Robert Stieve*

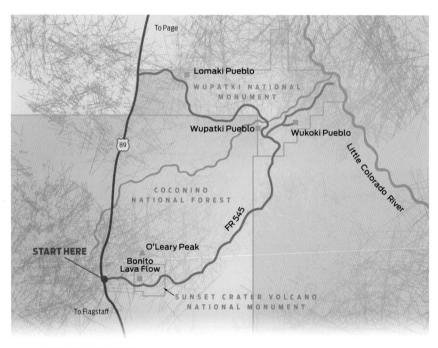

## TOUR GUIDE

**Note:** Mileages are approximate.

**Distance:** 73-mile loop (from Flagstaff)

**Directions:** From Flagstaff, go north on U.S. Route 89 for 12 miles to the Sunset Crater-Wupatki National Monument turnoff (Forest Road 545). Turn right onto FR 545 and continue 34.5 miles through both monuments, then back to U.S. 89. Turn left onto U.S. 89 and continue 26.5 miles back to Flagstaff.

**Vehicle requirements:** None

**Information:** Sunset Crater Volcano National Monument, 928-526-0502 or www.nps.gov/sucr; Wupatki National Monument, 928-679-2365 or www.nps.gov/wupa

## 12

# West Side Mormon Lake Road

**"B**etween every two pines is a doorway to a new world." So wrote the prolific adventurer and naturalist John Muir. If you're headed south from Flagstaff and want to prolong your stay in the pines, try West Side Mormon Lake Road (County Road 90). The ponderosas framing this 17-mile, partially paved route to Munds Park may not unlock fantasy worlds such as Narnia, but they will open myriad doorways to the mountains, where the magic of scent, shade and scenery prevails.

As a bonus, begin your journey just south of Flagstaff at Lake Mary Road, also known as Forest Highway 3 (Exit 339 off Interstate 17). The next 26 miles are scenic in their own right, with panoramic views of Lower and Upper Lake Mary — azure pools topped with lime-green patches and surrounded by indigo peaks. The lakes, created by twin dams in 1907, are named for the daughter of Flagstaff pioneer Timothy Riordan. Watch for bald eagles and ospreys that hunt near the water.

Follow the sign toward Dairy Springs

Gambel oaks mingle with ponderosa pines, forming a canopy over West Side Mormon Lake Road.
📷 ROBERT G. McDONALD

Lichen-covered boulders make up part of the landscape at the northern end of Mormon Lake.
📷 ROBERT G. MCDONALD

Campground, and turn right onto West Side Mormon Lake Road. Drive slowly as the road meanders toward the small town of Mormon Lake Village. Be mindful of pedestrians, horseback riders and campers.

About 3.5 miles down the road, look for Dairy Springs Campground, where Mormon settlers started a dairy farm in the late 1870s. The asphalt surrenders to dirt a mile later, at Forest Road 240. Turn right a few seconds before you get to the sign for Milepost 5. The bumpy road immediately angles uphill and crosses stands of Gambel oaks. After a mile, glance left for a clear view of ponderosas stretching to the horizon. Keep your eyes open for ATV users, who frequent the windy roads and surrounding forest. If you're lucky, you might also spot elk.

Pass a cattle guard and follow the road as it levels to the intersection of Forest Road 132A toward Mormon Mountain. Keep left to stay on FR 240. Another mile ahead, spindles of aspens intersperse with pines and create white gates to lower elevations. As sharp curves wend downhill, drive only as fast as your eyes can feast on fallen trees and the shrub-like New Mexico locust.

After 9 miles, continue right on FR 240 as it passes a farmhouse and spills onto spacious meadows. Crooked wooden fence posts guard wildflowers in the summer, along with the feathery-tipped grass known as foxtail barley. The next 6 miles make up a flat, easy drive through prairie lowlands frequented by prong-horns. The mahogany-colored road passes around the backside of the farmhouse and meets with Forest Road 700. Turn left to stay on FR 240, and follow it to the secluded Casner Park, named in honor of horse rancher Mose Casner, who lived near these quiet meadows in the 1880s. Here, mountain bluebirds flit between the pines, rustling the needles along with the breeze.

Steer over several humble hills and a dry wash to an iron gate, which marks FR 240's transition to a paved road called Pinewood Boulevard. The entrance to I-17 is about 2 miles down the road. The well-manicured Munds Park offers gas, food and a farewell glance at the pine-studded portals into the mountains.

— *Leah Duran*

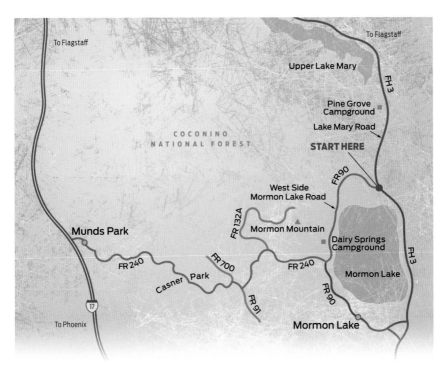

## TOUR GUIDE

**Note:** Mileages are approximate.

**Length:** 17 miles one way (from Lake Mary Road)

**Directions:** From Flagstaff, go southeast on Lake Mary Road (Forest Highway 3) for 26 miles, past Lower and Upper Lake Mary, to West Side Mormon Lake Road (County Road 90). Turn right onto West Side Mormon Lake Road and continue 5 miles to Forest Road 240. Turn right onto FR 240, which later turns into Pinewood Boulevard, and continue 12 miles to Munds Park and Interstate 17.

**Vehicle requirements:** None

**Information:** Flagstaff Ranger District, 928-526-0866 or www.fs.usda.gov/coconino

Along Perkinsville Road, an old railroad bridge crosses the Verde River on the way to Jerome.
GEORGE H.H. HUEY

# CENTRAL
# ARIZONA

# ·13

# Carefree to the Verde River

**S**heepherders never much liked the Verde River. In spring and fall, they had to swim their flocks across the water, leading them to summer pastures and winter ranges. It was dangerous business, and stray sheep often were lost to the river's current.

Finally, in 1944, the Flagstaff and Howard sheep companies completed construction of the Verde River Sheep Bridge, minimizing seasonal sheep loss and providing an easier entry to the west side of the Mazatzal Wilderness.

Today, a replica bridge crosses a portion of the Verde River north of Carefree, and it's the payoff to this scenic drive. But, like herding sheep across water, getting there takes a bit of work.

The route begins on the northeast outskirts of Carefree (just follow Cave Creek Road to the edge of town), a Phoenix suburb characterized by sprawling estates, cowboy-themed bars and plenty of antiques stores. As Cave Creek Road turns into Seven Springs Road after a half-mile, the route, which to this point has been bordered by mesquites, creosotes and the occasional paloverde, dips into a riparian area. Here, the green leaves of sycamores seem to burst out of the desert landscape.

At 0.8 miles, you'll pass the turnoff to Sears Kay Ruin, a Hohokam site that dates to 1500. It's a focal point along the Great Western Trail, of which this road is part. Notice the power lines that punctuate this route, and you'll scratch your head at

A replica of the original Verde River Sheep Bridge marks the conclusion of a drive from Carefree.
📷 GEORGE STOCKING

Saguaros and cottonwoods line a stream along the route to the Verde River.
📷 GEORGE STOCKING

the strange, sometimes-dysfunctional relationship between history, technology and nature.

Pavement ends at 2.6 miles, and the graded gravel road (now Forest Road 24) enters another riparian area before climbing again. Come spring, the hillsides that border the route will likely be awash with the wildflowers that carpet the Sonoran Desert — goldpoppies and lupines among them.

The drive continues past a few private properties and along boulders, fire-burned trees, prickly pear cactuses, saguaros and the occasional smattering of sacred datura for miles. Then, at Mile 9.5, it crosses Seven Springs and enters the Seven Springs Recreation Area. Here you'll find a campground constructed by the Civilian Conservation Corps in 1934. Just up the road, you'll find the Cave Creek Trailhead.

After the recreation area, FR 24 becomes narrower and a bit more rugged. It climbs again, and at Mile 14.3, you'll leave Maricopa County and enter Yavapai County. Almost immediately, grasses emerge along the roadside, the century plants appear a bit greener, and the datura blooms in abundance. Lockwood Mesa looms around Mile 16. You'll notice an unexpected little grove of dead trees about a mile and a half past the mesa.

Finally, the road branches at Mile 27.9, and you'll turn right onto Forest Road 269. Mesquite trees abound, and Tangle Peak rises on the left to an elevation of 3,542 feet. Wind-whipped junipers, groupings of saguaros and random cottonwoods are commonplace now, and they make the primitive, winding road more enjoyable. When you reach a cascade of boulders on the left side of the road at Mile 39.4, you'll know you're almost to the river. Then, after you pass the foundation of an old homestead at Mile 39.9, you'll see them — the bridge and the river.

Here, the road ends. Get out of the car, walk across the bridge and think of the sheepherders who came before you. To return to Carefree, retrace your route. Alternately, it's possible to travel FR 269 back the way you came, then continue west for another 27 miles through Agua Fria National Monument to Interstate 17.

If you choose the latter, you're in for a stunning trek, but it's a long one. Once you hit pavement again, you'll be ready to head home. And count some sheep.

— *Kelly Vaughn Kramer*

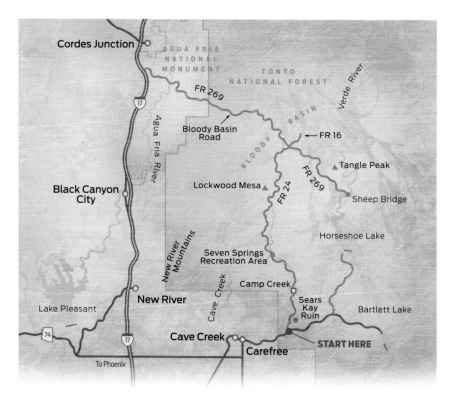

## TOUR GUIDE

**Note:** Mileages are approximate.

**Length:** 39.9 miles one way

**Directions:** From Carefree, go north on Cave Creek Road, which becomes Seven Springs Road (Forest Road 24), for 27.9 miles to Forest Road 269. Turn right onto FR 269 and continue 12 miles until the road ends at the Verde River Sheep Bridge.

**Vehicle requirements:** A high-clearance vehicle is required, and a four-wheel-drive vehicle is recommended for Forest Road 269. This route should not be attempted in inclement weather.

**Information:** Cave Creek Ranger District, 480-595-3300 or www.fs.usda.gov/tonto

# 14

# Cottonwood to Clarkdale

Everything old is new again. That phrase just about sums up the route from Cottonwood to Clarkdale, which follows three forest roads in the Verde Valley. The drive is all about seeing the very familiar from a very different vantage point.

This drive begins on Bill Gray Road (Forest Road 761), just off State Route 89A outside Cottonwood. After turning northwest onto FR 761, you'll pass the All Souls Cemetery. Veer right, and you'll spot a post with "761" etched on it. The rocky road is rough from the get-go and doesn't improve much until you reach the end, some 19 miles later. Take it easy as you get a feel

The route from Cottonwood to Clarkdale features sweeping views of the Verde Valley and Mingus Mountain in the Prescott National Forest.

📷 DEREK VON BRIESEN

Tuzigoot National Monument looms near the end of this drive, which ends at Tuzigoot Road.
📷 DEREK VON BRIESEN

for nature's potholes. The high-desert landscape is carpeted with spindly shrubs, cactuses and succulents. Meanwhile, the red rocks of Sedona will be on your right. There's something magical about seeing Sedona from this vantage point. The wide-angle perspective feels undisturbed, even serene — maybe it's the lack of car bumpers and brake lights.

For the next several miles, the road dips and rises repeatedly. The scenery shifts around Mile 4.5, when junipers appear in the landscape. As the road bends slightly west, the view of the red rocks gets interrupted around Mile 6 as power lines take center stage.

Just beyond the power lines, keep an eye out for a split in the road. The sign for Forest Road 258, which is your cue to turn left, is slightly obscured. After turning, you'll ascend a very rocky and narrow road. Around Mile 7, the route comes to a "T" junction. Veer right and continue on FR 258. As the road and surrounding landscape open up, out of nowhere, chalky limestone dominates the scenery. No wonder Verde Valley winemakers love the area — this is the kind of soil that produces crisp Arizona juice. The road eventually plateaus around Mile 9.7, where you'll be treated to a stunning view of Jerome, perched atop Cleopatra Hill. From there, the former mining colony has an Old World, fairy-tale quality about it that's more difficult to see when you approach it from SR 89A.

As the road winds down and around the hill and into the backcountry, you'll catch even more expansive views of the Verde Valley. By Mile 11, limestone gives way to clay, and in another 2 miles, you'll reach another "T" junction. Turn left onto Forest Road 131. As you descend into the valley, keep an eye out for oncoming traffic — blind driveways lead from nearby homes. By Mile 15, the road dips, and lush vegetation canopies the pavement as you near the Verde River around Mile 16. The route follows the narrow river as it slices its way past hillsides that bear scars from the area's early mining days. The road eventually turns to pavement at Mile 17, and after a brief climb, you'll spot Tuzigoot National Monument on the left. The drive comes to an abrupt end when it intersects with Tuzigoot Road. A left turn will take you to the ancient ruins. Turning right will take you into Clarkdale.

— *Kathy Ritchie*

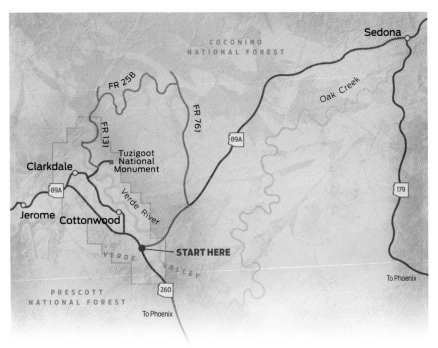

## TOUR GUIDE

**Note:** Mileages are approximate.

**Length:** 19.2 miles one way

**Directions:** From State Route 89A in Cottonwood, go north on Bill Gray Road (Forest Road 761) for 6.2 miles to Forest Road 258. Turn left onto FR 258 and continue 7 miles to Forest Road 131. Turn left onto FR 131 and continue 6 miles to Tuzigoot Road. Turn left to visit Tuzigoot National Monument or right to continue to Clarkdale.

**Vehicle requirements:** A four-wheel-drive vehicle is recommended, though the route is passable by a sedan in fair weather. Do not attempt the drive in inclement weather.

**Information:** Tuzigoot National Monument, 928-634-5564 or www.nps.gov/tuzi

# 15

# Florence-Kelvin Highway

**W**hen people think about Arizona's landscape, they typically think desert — a dusty, barren wasteland that's inhospitable at its worst and devoid of beauty at its best. It's a tough reputation to shake. After all, Arizona does have more than its share of arid land. In fact, it's home to 22.3 million acres of Sonoran Desert. And while it can be uninviting, it's also full of life, and one of the best places to see it is along the Florence-Kelvin Highway.

The 32-mile journey begins with a short run through a smattering of suburbia before arriving at the point where you'll need your camera. In fact, after turning east onto the Florence-Kelvin Highway from State Route 79, you might even wonder whether you veered the wrong way. Don't fret. In a matter of minutes, you'll see creosote bushes, chollas and ocotillos, and, depending on

Plants along the Florence-Kelvin Highway start their show of color as spring arrives.
📷 GEORGE STOCKING

Saguaros and paloverdes bloom along the route. Both plants usually bloom around the same time, between April and June.
📷 GEORGE STOCKING

the time of year, colorful wildflowers — in shades of yellow, red, orange and purple — that carpet the desert floor after heavy winter and spring rains. You'll also see saguaros, with their giant arms reaching toward the sky.

The desert road is paved for the first 12.3 miles before turning into graded dirt. It's an easy drive, and the traffic is usually light, allowing sightseers to literally stop and smell the wildflowers. At Mile 14.5, the road enters a box canyon (if the weather is inclement or rain is a possibility, don't enter) and turns sandy. But it's temporary. Once you're out of the canyon, it's back to gravel and those stunning Sonoran Desert views. The blue sky appears even more dramatic against the desert soil.

About a mile beyond the box canyon, after passing Barkerville Road, you'll spot an outcropping of boulders. It's a curious — and seemingly sudden — shift, and those dominant saguaros are dwarfed by the giant rocks that are piled on top of each other.

After crossing a cattle guard at Mile 18.8, the road opens up a little, and you might be tempted to speed up. But be careful. The road dips and unexpectedly goes from gravel to sand at times. The curves also become much sharper where the landscape morphs from vast, open desert to rugged mountain terrain on the approach to the Tortilla Mountains. In the distance, you'll see a huge gash in the mountainside, courtesy of an open-pit mine. You'll also catch a glimpse of a lush riparian area fed by the Gila River.

At Mile 27.7, the road passes the A-Diamond Ranch headquarters and begins to climb. Look to your right and you might see a stunning panorama of wildflowers.

By Mile 30, the journey nears its end, and before you know it, you're back on pavement. After crossing the Gila River on the one-lane bridge called the "Jake" Jacobson Bridge of Unity, you'll enter the tiny town of Kelvin, where the road connects with State Route 177.

— *Kathy Ritchie*

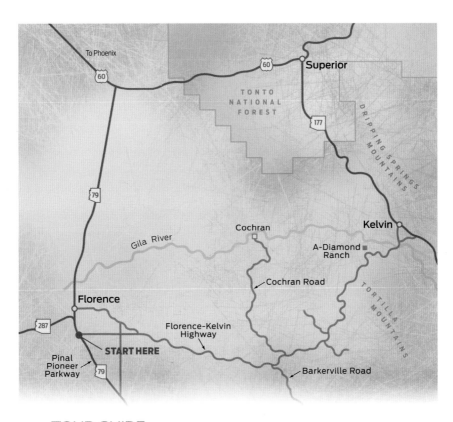

## TOUR GUIDE

**Note:** Mileages are approximate.

**Length:** 32 miles one way

**Directions:** From Phoenix, go east on U.S. Route 60 for 21 miles to State Route 79 (Pinal Pioneer Parkway). Turn right (south) onto SR 79 and continue 18 miles through Florence to the Florence-Kelvin Highway. Turn left (east) onto the Florence-Kelvin Highway and continue 32 miles to State Route 177.

**Vehicle requirements:** None

**Information:** Florence Visitors Center, 520-868-5216 or www.visitflorenceaz.com

# 16

# Forest Road 300

The Mogollon Rim. That's the biggest reason you'll want to make this drive. Although there are different opinions on how to pronounce the name — Spanish scholars go with "mo-go-yawn," locals use "muggy-on" — everyone agrees that "the Rim" is impressive.

Measured in thousands of feet and hundreds of miles, it's a massive wall of rock that begins near Arizona's border with New Mexico and stretches diagonally across most of the state. Through the lens of a camera, a set of binoculars or your own baby blues, the views from the top of the Rim are stunning, and on a clear day, you can see all the way to Mount Lemmon.

The vistas steal the show, but there's a lot to see along Forest Road 300, which can be approached from the east, near Woods Canyon Lake, or from the west, just north of Strawberry. This listing is written from the west, and it begins with an uphill climb through a thick pine forest — the Mogollon Rim is home to the world's largest stand of ponderosas. After 1.2 miles, FR 300 intersects what used to be the General Crook Trail, a historic wagon route that was used in the 1870s and 1880s to provide logistical support for General George Crook in the U.S. Army's war against the Apaches.

The Mogollon Rim features some of the most impressive vistas in Arizona.
◻ NICK BEREZENKO

Forest Road 300 dips into an aspen hollow as it approaches Woods Canyon Lake.
📷 NICK BEREZENKO

From there, the gravel road winds downhill to an area of grassy meadows crowded with tall evergreens. It's a beautiful place to pitch a tent. Hardwoods and spruce start mixing in after that. You'll also start seeing the first of many worthwhile side trips: Potato Lake, Lee Johnson Spring, Kehl Springs Campground. Then, after 7.5 miles, you'll get to the dead zone of the Dude Fire.

The fire was sparked by a bolt of lightning on June 25, 1990, and within a few hours, it had become one of the deadliest and most destructive fires in Arizona history. In addition to the obliteration of more than 24,000 acres, six firefighters lost their lives. Only the Yarnell Hill Fire (June 2013) was worse in that regard. Today, the effects of the Dude Fire are still obvious. There's very little new growth, other than grass, but the long views to the south help mitigate the damage.

Also, the fire zone makes up only a small stretch of FR 300, and at the 10.2-mile mark you'll leave it behind and re-enter the beautiful. The rest of the route epitomizes the purity of nature, and still measures up to Captain George M. Wheeler's description of the Rim in the late 1800s: "Mountain, forest, valley and streams are blended in one harmonious whole," he wrote. "Few worldwide travelers in a lifetime could be treated to a more perfect landscape, a true virgin solitude, undefiled by the presence of man."

Heading east, that perfect landscape includes Crackerbox Canyon and the Arizona Trail, one of several great hikes on the Rim. Another keeper is the Houston Brothers Trail, which shows up after 16.2 miles. Barbershop Canyon is just beyond that, followed by the Myrtle Trail and turnoffs to Lost Lake and Knoll Lake. Add them to the list of great side trips.

Moving on, about 25 miles in, the Rim Road, as it's known, crosses from the Coconino National Forest into the Apache-Sitgreaves National Forests. The transition isn't important except that it coincides with a large meadow dotted with young ponderosas. It's nice to see the new growth. The upper trailhead for Horton Springs is ahead on your right, and a few miles later, you'll arrive at the turnoff for Bear Canyon Lake, one of the Rim's premier recreation areas — go for the camping, hiking and fishing. Of all the detours, this one deserves some real consideration.

Aspens, evergreens and panoramas mark the home stretch to Woods Canyon Lake, where the scenic drive comes to an end. You won't want it to end, though. In fact, if you could pick one place to break down, get lost or drop out, Forest Road 300 would be it. Wildlife sightings (elk and mule deer in particular) are common, the cool pine forest is refreshing, the vistas are remarkable ... no matter how you pronounce it, the Mogollon Rim is one of the most scenic drives anywhere.

— *Robert Stieve*

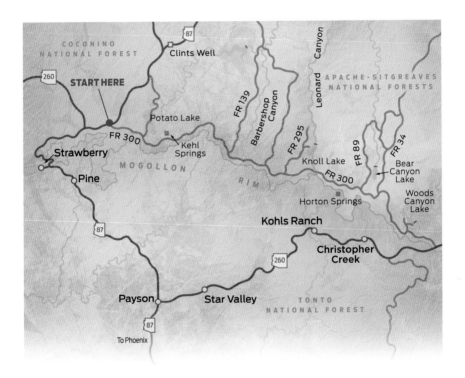

## TOUR GUIDE

**Note:** Mileages are approximate.
**Length:** 43.3 miles one way
**Directions:** From Payson, go north on State Route 87 for 28.5 miles to Forest Road 300. Turn right onto FR 300 and continue 43.3 miles to State Route 260.
**Vehicle requirements:** None
**Information:** Mogollon Rim Ranger District, 928-477-2255 or www.fs.usda.gov/coconino; Black Mesa Ranger District, 928-535-7300 or www.fs.usda.gov/asnf

# 17

# Joshua Tree Parkway

**W**hen Mormon settlers first saw the plant they dubbed the "Joshua tree," it reminded them of the bushy-bearded biblical leader. When Territorial Governor John C. Frémont caught sight of it during an 1844 trek through the Mohave Desert, he called it "the most repulsive tree in the vegetable kingdom."

Here's the thing: Joshua trees are not vegetables and they're not among the 12 spies of Israel, but they are members of the agave family. What's more, they're plentiful along U.S. Route 93 from Wikieup to Wickenburg.

The drive, which is familiar to anyone who's road-tripped from Phoenix to Sin City (or vice versa), officially begins in Wikieup, a dot on the map that's better known for its pie (you'll pass Luchia's) than for its tourism cachet. Other landmarks "in town" include

The twisting arms of Joshua trees dominate the desert landscape along the road between Wikieup and Wickenburg.
📷 NEIL WEIDNER

The stretch of U.S. Route 93 from Wikieup to Wickenburg features stunning scenery.
📷 NEIL WEIDNER

the Snoopy-piloted Wikieup arrow, along with the Wikieup Trading Post and the creosote-peppered hills that surround Bronco Wash.

Heading south on U.S. 93, around Milepost 127, you'll come to the Big Sandy River, and unless it's been raining, the river is probably just that — big and sandy. Beyond the Big Sandy, sheer, eroded cliffs loom, speckled in spots with saguaros and scrub. Pale, striated canyon walls straddle the highway — green, yellow, white and taupe — and the mountains stretch for miles in front of you.

At Milepost 147, you'll start seeing rocks piled on top of each other. They look like hoodoos, with saguaros in between. The rocks are an interesting sight, but not as interesting as Nothing. Blink and you'll miss it, but Nothing was a real Arizona town, and you'll see it off to the left. It's marked with a sign and a pile of ... well, junk. You'll have to see it for yourself, but Nothing really is something.

Joshua trees become the focal point of this drive around Milepost 162. One of the first you'll see is a large, gnarly fellow off to the right, and then several more in rapid succession. They're reminiscent of the baobab trees made famous in Antoine de Saint-Exupéry's *The Little Prince*, and if your imagination is active, you might see a little blond boy emerge from the trees with a dog and a well-protected flower in hand.

By Milepost 169, the forest of Joshua trees is dense, and you'll see a sign that reads, "Joshua Tree Parkway of Arizona." It's a label that formalizes the obvious — that this is an incredibly scenic drive that passes through one of the most spectacular landscapes in the Southwest. The route continues on to Wickenburg, a classic Old West town that celebrates the state's cowboy heritage with the Desert Caballeros Museum and a string of Western-themed shops and restaurants. It's a great place to visit, but the highlight of this drive is the trees. Or, rather, the agaves.

— *Kelly Vaughn Kramer*

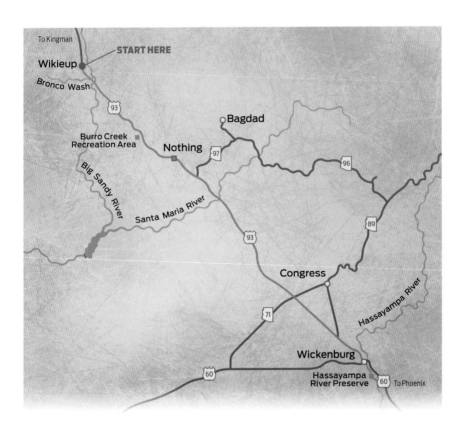

## TOUR GUIDE

**Note:** Mileages are approximate.
**Length:** 74 miles one way
**Directions:** From Wikieup, travel south on U.S. Route 93 for 74 miles to Wickenburg.
**Vehicle Requirements:** None
**Information:** Arizona Scenic Roads, www.arizonascenicroads.com

# 18

# Perkinsville Road

**M**ountain man Bill Williams, rancher Marion Perkins and investor Eugene Jerome never met, but they're connected by two things. The first is that they all lent their names to Northern Arizona burgs. The second is the wildly scenic Perkinsville Road, which slices through the historically well-trodden, currently forgotten countryside between their namesake towns.

Williams — a rough-and-tumble ranching, lumber and railway center appropriately named after a rugged adventurer — fell into decline in the last century. Twice. First, with the demise of the Atchison, Topeka and Santa Fe Railway; second, when it became the last Historic Route 66 town to be bypassed by Interstate 40. Currently, as the southern terminus of the Grand Canyon Railway, it's experiencing a minor renaissance.

Begin this 47-mile drive in the colorful historic district of restored saloons and bordellos, heading south on Fourth Street, which becomes Perkinsville Road, also marked as County Road 73.

The first stretch meanders through the Kaibab National Forest, passing the occasional llama ranch and aspen grove. At about 11 miles, the elevation

The one-lane Perkinsville Bridge crosses the Verde River as Perkinsville Road approaches Jerome.
📷 TOM BROWNOLD

Perkinsville Road is ideal for viewing wildflowers and the changing colors of aspen groves.
📷 PAUL GILL

slowly decreases, and with it, the height of the pine trees, which now mingle with juniper, oak and mesquite. Flat-topped Mingus Mountain looms into view, seeming so far away it's hard to believe it's your destination.

Once you leave Coconino County and enter Yavapai County, the road becomes County Road 70. At 24 miles, the pavement ends, but the road is still suitable for a regular passenger vehicle in good weather. After 3 miles on the dirt road, turn right onto County Road 72 (still Perkinsville Road), which wends its way toward Perkinsville.

Despite earning a dot on a map, Perkinsville is not so much a town as ... well, a ranch. But what it lacks in population, it makes up for in big scenery. It's easy to see why, in 1900, the Perkins family put down roots in this pastoral landscape of grama grass backdropped by endless blue sky. The perennial Verde River burbles through, flanked by cottonwoods that, in the fall, resemble giant yellow cauliflowers.

You'll traverse the one-lane Perkinsville Bridge — the most reliable crossing on the Verde River, and a put-in point for rafters. A sign directs you to Jerome along much the same route as the one the Perkinses used to transport their beef to feed the town's miners in the early 1900s. Past Perkinsville, the landscape becomes a dry series of gray hillocks patched with yellow grasses and spattered with juniper.

Shortly, the road turns and changes dramatically. These last few miles are not for the acrophobic or lead-footed. You'll be negotiating a winding, gravelly one-lane road carved out of the hills that follow the old bed of the United Verde & Pacific Railway. There's no guardrail to prevent cars from plummeting off the cliff, which is frustrating, given the views that tempt your eyes off the road. The whole valley spreads out below, with beige hills undulating into Sedona's red rocks and Humphreys Peak standing blue on the horizon. Then there's the unique opportunity of approaching the mile-high hill town of Jerome from above.

New York investor Eugene Jerome never saw his namesake town — not when it was teeming with miners and prostitutes at the turn of the century, and certainly not these days, when it's teeming with artists, tourists and flotillas of Harley-Davidsons.

Like the town of Williams, Jerome is a wild child made good, a Western town that's followed a familiar boom/bust/baby-boom pattern. We'll never know what adventurous trapper Bill Williams, pioneering rancher Marion Perkins and copper-mining mogul Eugene Jerome would think of the decline of their industries and the taming of this chunk of the Wild West. But it's something to ponder, perhaps over a famous cheeseburger at the Haunted Hamburger, where you can finally savor those valley views from the safety of the balcony.

— *Keridwen Cornelius*

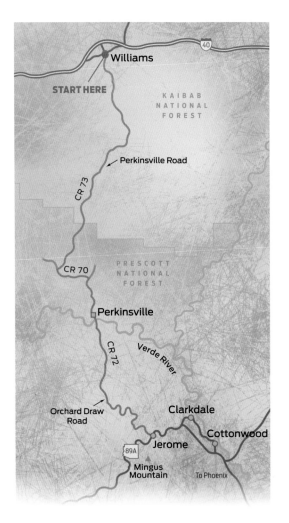

## TOUR GUIDE

**Note:** Mileages are approximate.

**Distance:** 47 miles one way

**Directions:** From Williams, go south on Fourth Street, which becomes Perkinsville Road (County Road 73) and later turns into County Road 70, for 27 miles to County Road 72. Turn right onto CR 72 and continue 20 miles to Jerome.

**Vehicle requirements:** None in good weather, but a four-wheel-drive vehicle is recommended during winter, when snow may be on the road, and in July or August, when afternoon thunderstorms are common.

**Information:** Williams Chamber of Commerce, 800-863-0546 or www.experience williams.com; Jerome Chamber of Commerce, 928-634-2900 or www.jerome chamber.com

# 19

# Pinal
# Mountains
# Loop

**C**rawl. Walk. Run. The evolution of human movement seems simple enough. But it's a formula that also can be applied to other, non-bipedal modes of getting from one place to another — like driving. Creep. Cruise. Fly.

In the case of this drive, which curls in a loop through the Pinal Mountains near Globe, you'll be tempted to fly. Instead — thanks to the ruggedness of the road (yes, you need a four-wheel-drive) and the draw of the scenery — you're better off cruising, even creeping, in parts.

The route begins on Icehouse Canyon Road (Forest Road 112), in a residential area just beyond

Sotol flowers and century plants dominate the scenery along the Pinal Mountains Loop.
📷 RICK GIASE

Globe's Besh-Ba-Gowah Archaeological Park contains ruins of pueblos about 800 years old.
📷 RICHARD MAACK

Besh-Ba-Gowah Archaeological Park. After 3.7 miles, you'll see a sign for the Tonto National Forest. Here, civilization fades away, left to the telephone lines, homes and corrals you've experienced up to this point. Manzanita, scrubby bushes and an occasional juniper comprise the landscape, and around Mile 4.7, you'll come upon a view of Cobre Valley out the driver's-side window. It's marked by a cascade of granite boulders and will likely be commemorated through an "Oh, look at that" from you or one of your passengers.

As the road climbs, pine trees replace the scrub, though manzanita bushes remain commonplace throughout the drive. The pines get taller and the shadows grow deeper around Mile 7.2 as the forest thickens, and the well-maintained dirt road passes through the Pioneer Pass Recreation Area at Mile 8.6. Here, you'll find restrooms and a place to stretch your legs. It's also a great place to gather your wits, crack your knuckles and gird your belly for the remainder of the drive.

Once you're past the recreation area, the road grows rockier — wilder, in a sense — and you may encounter an occasional grouping of bright-orange or red wildflowers as it descends toward Pioneer Basin. Around Mile 10.8, you'll see the radio towers atop Signal Peak and begin cruising through more high-desert landscape. A mile later, you'll come to a turnoff. You can go straight for Pioneer Basin, but, for the purposes of this drive, turn right onto Forest Road 221 at the sign for the Bobtail Ridge Trail and Doak Spring.

A couple of miles past the turn, you'll see a sign for Pioneer Pass, but veer right to stay on FR 221. Hillsides of agaves and century plants become the primary scenery along this section of the drive, but you'll want to keep your eyes peeled for a variety of birds and white-tailed deer, which are common in this area.

The road turns and climbs, then descends, twists and turns again in this neck of the woods, and there will be moments when you won't be able to anticipate what's over the next ridge or beyond the next curve. It's four-wheel-drive in these parts, and that's why it's important to creep while you're on FR 221.

Around Mile 18.5, you'll come to a burned hillside, the remnant of some long-ago fire. If it's cloudy, the skeletons of trees will look eerie against the backdrop of a storm, but shortly thereafter, the valley stretches like a canvas.

You'll come to a fork in the road just shy of Mile 20. Turn left onto Forest Road

651 and veer left, then quickly right, when you come to another fork less than a half-mile later. This road is a well-maintained respite after the primitive stretch of FR 221, and you'll appreciate the pretty recreation area it runs through, rich with sycamores and oaks. After a 5-mile cruise along FR 651, you'll turn right (east) onto Kellner Canyon Road (Forest Road 55) to return to Icehouse Canyon Road. Feel free to fly — within reason, at or under the speed limit.

— *Kelly Vaughn Kramer*

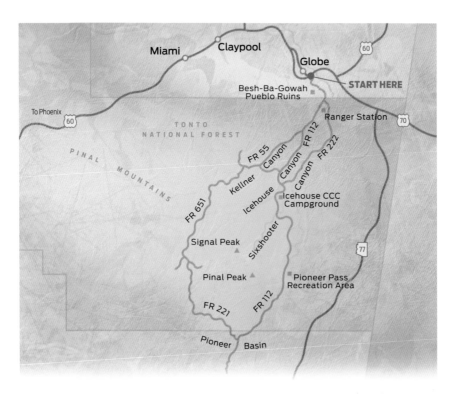

## TOUR GUIDE

**Note:** Mileages are approximate.

**Length:** 30.5-mile loop

**Directions:** From Globe, follow the signs toward Besh-Ba-Gowah Pueblo Ruins. Just past the turnoff, turn right onto Icehouse Canyon Road (Forest Road 112) and go south for 11.8 miles to Forest Road 221. Turn right onto FR 221 and continue 8 miles to Forest Road 651. Turn left onto FR 651 and continue 0.3 miles. From there, veer left, then take an immediate right to stay on FR 651. Continue on FR 651 for an additional 5 miles to Kellner Canyon Road (Forest Road 55). Turn right onto Kellner Canyon Road and continue 2.5 miles back to Icehouse Canyon Road. Turn left onto Icehouse Canyon Road and continue 2.9 miles back to the starting point.

**Vehicle requirements:** A high-clearance, four-wheel-drive vehicle is required.

**Information:** Globe Ranger District, 928-402-6200 or www.fs.usda.gov/tonto

# 20

# Prescott to Camp Wood

**B**oth ends of this drive are scenic, but the nature of that scenery — from Prescott's small-town charm to Camp Wood's quiet isolation — couldn't be more different. You'll need a reliable vehicle and a three-hour block of time, but that's a small price to pay for the varied and breathtaking views you'll find on this drive.

Reset your trip odometer at the northwest corner of Courthouse Square in downtown Prescott, a town that served two stints as the Territorial capital in the second half of the 19th century. Today, Prescott is known, in part, for Whiskey Row, its historic area of bars and restaurants. It's a great place to grab lunch before beginning the drive.

As you head west, you'll end up on Williamson Valley Road, which winds north past the horse and cattle ranches on the outskirts of town. To the east is Granite Mountain (7,626 feet), and at Mile 9, you'll pass the Williamson Valley Trailhead, from which several moderate hiking trails can be accessed. Five miles past that, keep an eye out on the right for a glimpse of the San Francisco Peaks near

Open grassland lines Williamson Valley Road along the route to Camp Wood.
📷 NICK BEREZENKO

Pronghorns are a common sight along the route, but you'll need to be quick with your camera.
📷 NICK BEREZENKO

Flagstaff. You'll see more of the peaks later, but for now, the road descends into a more forested area.

Open grasslands, small trees and the occasional windmill dominate the view as you continue on. When Williamson Valley Road runs out of pavement, it's time to turn onto Forest Road 21 (labeled as County Road 68 on some maps), a dirt road that climbs into the Prescott National Forest to the west. Early on, a sign warns you to watch for animals. If you're lucky, you might see a herd of pronghorns, often mistaken for antelopes, grazing near the roadside. The pronghorn is the continent's fastest land animal, so have your camera ready.

Around Mile 30, the grasslands give way to ponderosa pines as you head deeper into the forest. There are several great views on both sides as you continue on, so take it slow — which you should be doing anyway, because the road gets rougher and narrower as you gain elevation. There isn't much traffic here, but be ready to pull to the side for oncoming vehicles. And don't leave without pulling over at Mile 33 to enjoy the panorama of the small valley below.

The drive concludes at Camp Wood, the site of a cavalry post during the Territorial days. There's nothing left of the camp but a large clearing, and it's a good place to stretch your legs and debate your next move. If you're driving a high-clearance vehicle, you can head north on Forest Road 95 to Walnut Creek, 11 miles away, and make your way to Prescott from there. Otherwise, retrace your route on FR 21 and Williamson Valley Road. If you choose the latter, watch for another incredible view of the San Francisco Peaks shortly after you start the drive back. You'll know it when you see it.

— *Noah Austin*

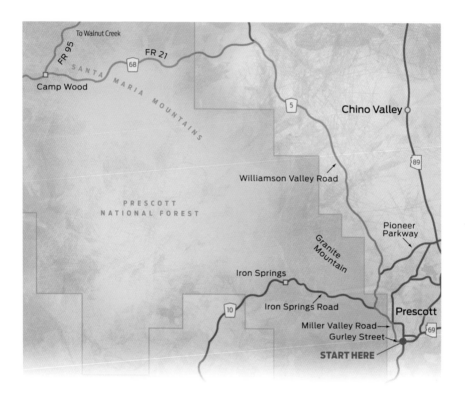

## TOUR GUIDE

**Note:** Mileages are approximate

**Length:** 41 miles one way

**Directions:** From the northwest corner of Courthouse Square in Prescott, go west on Gurley Street for 0.4 miles to Grove Avenue. Turn right onto Grove Avenue, which turns into Miller Valley Road, and continue 1.2 miles to Iron Springs Road. Turn left onto Iron Springs Road and continue 1.4 miles to Williamson Valley Road. Turn right onto Williamson Valley Road and continue 22 miles to Forest Road 21 (labeled as County Road 68 on some maps). Turn left onto FR 21 and continue 16 miles to the Camp Wood site, on the right.

**Vehicle requirements:** A high-clearance vehicle is recommended, but FR 21 is passable in a standard sedan in good weather.

**Information:** Chino Valley Ranger District, 928-777-2200 or www.fs.usda.gov/prescott

# 21

# Queen Valley Road

**R**elationships are funny things. To make them work, you have to compromise. The same rule can be applied to scenic drives. Some scenic drives, anyway. Queen Valley Road in the Superstition Mountains is a good example. If you're like my driving companion, Jon, who loves the adrenaline rush that comes from plowing across boulder-strewn terrain, then you'll love the second half of this drive. It requires four-wheel-drive, which makes me nervous, because all I can think about in those scenarios is driving off a cliff. If you're like-minded and prefer stunning views to white-knuckle switchbacks, then the first half of this trek will be right up your alley.

After turning left onto Queen Valley Road off of

Queen Valley Road, which runs through the Superstition Mountains, pairs scenic desert landscapes with narrow switchbacks.
📷 GEORGE STOCKING

Cottonwoods and saguaros dot a hillside along a wash in the Superstition Mountains.
📷 GEORGE STOCKING

U.S. Route 60 east of Phoenix, we drive more than a mile before turning right onto Forest Road 357 (Hewitt Station Road), which is where we zero out the odometer to officially measure this scenic drive. The road meanders for a good 2 miles before hitting Forest Road 172, on the left. The turnoff is well marked but requires some attention — there are several offshoot roads for quads and bikes. The dirt road quickly narrows, and at Mile 3.5, we come to a fork. Unsure, we veer right.

The landscape is at once brutal and beautiful. Owl's-clover and Mexican gold-poppies are juxtaposed against the harsh, jagged hills. Around Mile 5.3, we drop deeper into the Superstitions' inner sanctum. As the canyon walls close in around us, layers of rock appear otherworldly. Spindly cactuses cover the rocky hillsides, and saguaros stand like sentinels at the edge of the road. Their arms hang over us like protective giants. We're on Mother Nature's turf, and it's divine.

By Mile 14, the saguaros are gone, replaced by piñon pines and juniper bushes, which cover the hillsides. A tight switchback at Mile 15.9 forces us to pull over and make a three-point turn. The road looks gnarly, so we decide it's time for four-wheel-drive. As we continue our climb — vertically — we come to a "T" junction and veer right onto Forest Road 650. At this point, the road is practically impassable without four-wheel-drive. As we crawl over small boulders, the road narrows, and navigating it requires some finesse. Jon is in his element and loves every moment. Fists clenched, I decide compromise is for the birds.

Around Mile 20, we see remnants of a fire. Contorted branches that look like witches' fingers reach out and scratch our SUV. The narrow road ahead hugs the mountainside like a ribbon. There's no room for another vehicle to pass — and no guardrail.

The next 10 miles feel endless as we begin our descent down a rocky hill made up of nauseatingly tight switchbacks. At Mile 24.9, we come to another "T" junction. There are no signs, so we turn right and hope for the best. After crossing several sandy washes, we spot U.S. 60 up ahead. After 33 miles, we're finally back on pavement. Jon comes down from his adrenaline high, and my stomach slowly settles.

"That was awesome," Jon says.

"Yep," I reply. "That first part was really stunning."

— *Kathy Ritchie*

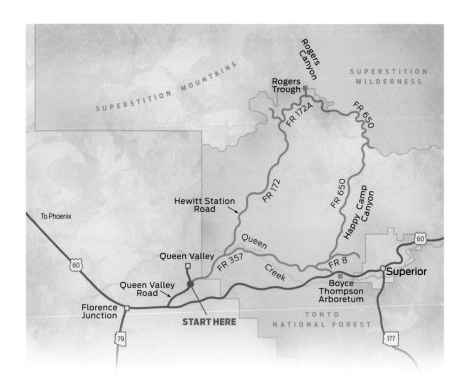

## TOUR GUIDE

**Note:** Mileages are approximate.

**Length:** 33 miles one way

**Directions:** From Phoenix, go east on U.S. Route 60 for 43 miles to Queen Valley Road. Turn left onto Queen Valley Road and continue 2 miles to Forest Road 357 (Hewitt Station Road). Turn right onto FR 357 and continue 3 miles to Forest Road 172. Turn left onto FR 172 and continue 13 miles to Forest Road 650. Turn right onto FR 650 and continue 15 miles to Forest Road 8. Turn right onto FR 8 and continue 2 miles to FR 357. Turn left onto FR 357 and continue less than a quarter-mile to U.S. 60.

**Vehicle requirements:** A high-clearance, four-wheel-drive vehicle is required.

**Information:** Mesa Ranger District, 480-610-3300 or www.fs.usda.gov/tonto

The Coronado Trail winds past some of Arizona's most beautiful spots, including Hannagan Meadow.

RANDY PRENTICE

98

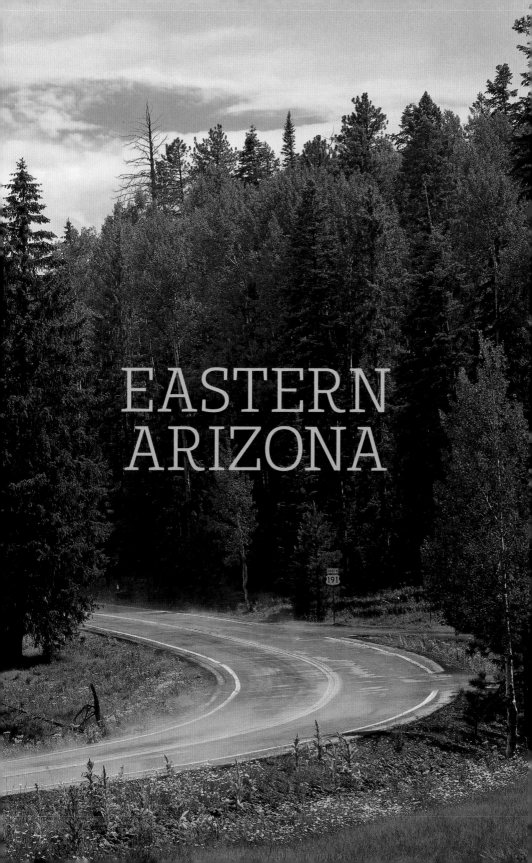

EASTERN
ARIZONA

# 22

# Black Hills Back Country Byway

**C**ruising among the Black Hills near Safford, it's easy to get carried away in an imaginary game of cowboys and Indians. Patches of prickly pear cactuses and fields of native grasses cover the talus slopes, which were crafted by volcanic activity more than 20 million years ago. The foliage would make for some seriously great cover should a battle break out — or, better yet, a pretty prickly corner into which the enemy could be backed. Either way, it's easy to see why Geronimo wandered these hills during raids into Mexico and back.

The 21-mile drive begins at its southern point, off of U.S. Route 191, approximately 20 miles east of Safford. You'll turn left onto the Black Hills Back Country Byway, a gravel road that's maintained by Graham and Greenlee counties. Although a four-wheel-drive vehicle isn't necessary — unless you plan to explore one of the numerous side roads along the way — a high-clearance vehicle is recommended.

Prison laborers built the byway

Mexican goldpoppies surround prickly pear cactuses in the Black Hills near Safford.
TOM DANIELSEN

The Old Safford Bridge spans the Gila River along the Black Hills Back Country Byway.
📷 GEORGE STOCKING

between 1914 and 1920, during which a few managed to escape. Most, however, behaved. Just as the hillsides are great for a Wild West game of hide-and-seek, they're also foreboding. If you venture outside the car for a closer look, be sure to keep your eyes peeled for rattlesnakes and other desert critters.

Several interpretive areas pepper the route, and there are other potential stops along the way. The first comes approximately 3 miles into the drive, where the road crests above the Twin C Ranch. There, you can take a side trip to the Black Hills Rockhound Area in search of fire agate or continue past an abandoned mine. Just down the road, a cinder pit looms red and dusty against the onyx hills. In the 1950s, miners pulled pumice from the pit and trucked it to Safford, where it was converted into cinder blocks.

This is a good spot to look up. On a crisp, clear day, a swath of mountain-studded desert paints the horizon, and the Dos Cabezas Mountains rise a scant 50 miles away. From there, the road climbs steadily into the hills as chollas and bursts of yuccas punctuate the abundant prickly pears. The road reaches its highest point near the 12-mile mark, then descends in a series of twists and turns.

The remnants of the labor camp, where the prisoners rested each evening, are a quick walk from the roadside between mileposts 16 and 17. The old structures are nothing special — just block and rebar — but they do speak to the ruggedness of the terrain. Life in the Black Hills at the beginning of the 20th century couldn't have been easy. Mining was big here during Arizona's boom days, when cotton and copper were king in this neck of the woods, and it still is today — the Freeport-McMoRan open-pit copper mine in Morenci is a fitting reminder of that.

The road winds back to U.S. 191 after traversing the Old Safford Bridge, which crosses the Gila River. The bridge, constructed in 1918, doesn't look a day over 32 — partly because it was restored several years ago. Just below the bridge is a popular place to launch rafts and kayaks to float the 23 miles of river in the Gila Box Riparian National Conservation Area. Past the bridge, the Bureau of Land Management's Owl Creek Campground provides views of the river and riparian area below.

— *Kelly Vaughn Kramer*

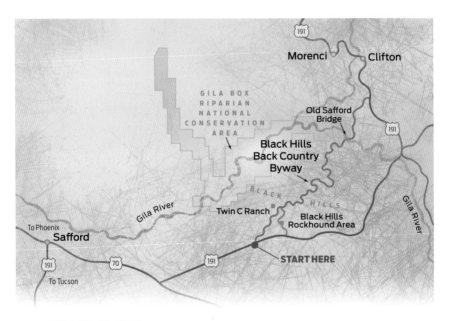

## TOUR GUIDE

**Note:** Mileages are approximate.

**Length:** 21 miles one way

**Directions:** From Safford, go east on U.S. Route 70, which runs concurrently with U.S. Route 191, for 10 miles, until the two routes split. Turn left (north) onto U.S. 191 and continue 10 miles to the Black Hills Back Country Byway entrance (near Milepost 139). Turn left onto the byway and continue 21 miles to its northern junction with U.S. 191.

**Vehicle requirements:** A high-clearance vehicle is recommended. A four-wheel-drive vehicle is required to travel the roads that branch from the byway.

**Information:** Bureau of Land Management, Safford Field Office, 928-348-4400 or www.blm.gov/az

# 23

# Coronado Trail

If you're familiar with *Arizona Highways*, you'll know that we've been down this road before. Of course we have. *Arizona Highways* has been covering the scenic wonders of the state since 1925, so it stands to reason that Arizona's version of "the long and winding road" would have found its way into the magazine on many occasions. That said, it's always worth another look, and no book of scenic drives would be complete without this one. Like the Beatles' swan song, this road trip is a classic.

Designated a National Scenic Byway in 2005, the Coronado Trail winds for more than a hundred miles from the twin cities of Eagar and Springerville in the north to the twin cities of Clifton and Morenci in the south. In between, the four-hour route follows the trail

The remote Hannagan Meadow, along the Coronado Trail, is an ideal stargazing location.
📷 JEFF KIDA

The East Fork of the Black River flows through the Black Mountains.

📷 RANDY PRENTICE

used in 1540 by Spanish explorer Francisco Vásquez de Coronado as he searched for the fabled "Seven Cities of Cibola." He wasn't joy-riding in an Escalade, but he surely marveled at the views, which begin among the rolling grasslands on the outskirts of Eagar.

From there, the southbound route climbs past the Sipe White Mountain Wildlife Area — look for elk, ospreys and golden eagles — into the spruce-fir forests near Alpine, a Swiss-like village settled in the late 1870s. Along the way you're going to confront the harsh realities of what happens when Leave No Trace ethics are ignored. The Wallow Fire, which was started in 2011 by two careless campers from Tucson, torched nearly 540,000 acres of gorgeous forest, including most of Escudilla Mountain (Aldo Leopold is surely rolling in his grave). Some of the worst evidence of the fire can be seen from the road just before Alpine.

Despite the carnage, the overall drive is still remarkable, and even the burn areas are coming back to life as a result of the lush grasses and young aspens that are moving in. Nevertheless, please use your ashtray. Not just on this drive, but everywhere.

Just south of Alpine, which is the last stop for fuel, you'll come to Hannagan Meadow. Named for Robert Hannagan, a Nevada miner who did some cattle-ranching in the area, the meadow would have certainly inspired a Frost poem, had he ever walked by.

In a place as beautiful as this, you might expect to see a string of B&Bs, hotels, motels, RV parks and campgrounds. But you won't. The only thing around is Hannagan Meadow Lodge, which stands alone in the middle of the Apache National Forest, a place generally off-limits to commercial development. The remote address is the main attraction, but the lodge itself is nice, too.

Surrounding the lodge is the Blue Range Primitive Area, which offers some of the most incredible scenery in the state. Among the highlights are three beautiful rivers — the Black, the Blue and the San Francisco.

As you head south, keep your eyes peeled. Within a stone's throw of the road are more than 100 species of fish and wildlife, including elk, mule deer, pronghorns, black bears, squirrels, bald eagles and 160 other kinds of birds. The fishing is great, and the stands of aspens, oaks, maples, mountain ash, firs, spruce and junipers will make wherever you came from seem like a million miles away.

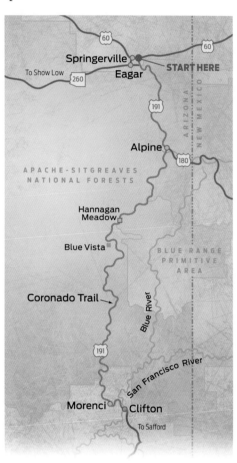

Like many roads in Arizona, the Coronado Trail is a four-season wonderland. Fall colors are incredible. Spring wildflowers are spectacular. Winter snows make the area the state's cross-country skiing mecca. And in summer, the cool temperatures speak for themselves.

The next stop is the Blue Vista rest stop at the edge of the Mogollon Rim, which, on a clear day, allows you to see as far as the eye can see. From there, the road works its way south to Clifton and Morenci, and tests your nerve with some hair-raising curves. Although the twin cities at the end of the road aren't as scenic as their sisters in the north — open-pit mining has a way of doing that — they do have an important history, along with some of the nicest people you'll ever meet. The towns have gas stations, too, which will come in handy if you decide to turn around. And you probably will. As you'll see, the long and winding road is always worth another look.

— *Robert Stieve*

## TOUR GUIDE

**Note:** Mileages are approximate.

**Distance:** 120 miles one way

**Directions:** From Payson, go east on State Route 260 for 87 miles to U.S. Route 60. Turn left onto U.S. 60 and continue 49 miles to Springerville. From Springerville, go south on U.S. Route 191 for 120 miles to Clifton.

**Vehicle requirements:** None, but there are several sharp curves and steep drop-offs along this narrow road — in some cases, there are no guardrails, and in some areas, speeds may slow to 10 mph.

**Information:** Alpine Ranger District, 928-339-5000 or www.fs.usda.gov/asnf

# 24

# Eagar to Big Lake

In Arizona, there's no better reminder of the importance of proper campfire management than the remnants of the Wallow Fire. The blaze started when an abandoned campfire spread to nearby trees, and it ultimately burned nearly 540,000 acres and became the largest recorded wildfire in the state's history. Although you will see a few signs of Wallow's devastation along this 21-mile, back-road route to Big Lake, you'll also see swaths of grasslands, crystal-clear water and myriad reminders that the White Mountains are still spectacular.

The drive begins at the only traffic signal in Eagar, a small town that was first settled in 1871. As you head south, you'll find yourself on Forest Road 285. The road is dirt, but it's well maintained. If you're traveling in a sedan, you'll easily navigate FR 285 in good weather.

The road quickly climbs to an elevation of about 9,000 feet, so keep in mind that pockets of snow and ice may be present,

Aspens line the shore of Big Lake, the tranquil conclusion to a back-road drive from Eagar.
NICK BEREZENKO

Forest Road 285 (Water Canyon Road) approaches Crosby Crossing on its way from Eagar to Big Lake.
📷 NICK BEREZENKO

even in summer. And it narrows to one lane in places, so watch for oncoming traffic and remember that if you come face to face with another motorist, the car traveling uphill has the right of way.

You'll soon enter the Apache-Sitgreaves National Forests, where ponderosa pines, smaller evergreens and spindly, dance-in-the-wind aspens dominate the roadside as you wind your way into the forest. This is ungulate country, so take your time around the many blind corners — you never know when an elk might saunter across the road.

Aspens become more abundant as you gain elevation, and 10 miles in, the forest gives way to the first of several large meadows. The uninterrupted horizon to the southwest offers a good view of Mount Baldy. Baldy, one of the highest peaks in Arizona — its summit reaches 11,400 feet — is sacred to the Western Apache people, and its Apache name translates to "White Mountain," which is easily understood by anyone who has seen it in the middle of winter.

A fairly constant breeze wafts over the meadows, so pull off the road, silence the sedan and enjoy the mountain air. If you're lucky, you might see an animal — ungulate, turkey or otherwise — taking a drink at one of the many ponds near the roadside.

The last few miles of FR 285 plunge back into heavy forest, and although you'll see a few areas where Wallow left its mark, a right turn onto Forest Road 249 takes you about 2 miles to Big Lake, one of the best lakes for fishing in Arizona and a great location for summer camping.

With a surface area of 450 acres, the lake is populated by rainbow, brook and cutthroat trout, which are stocked regularly by the Arizona Game and Fish Department. The lake's five campgrounds are popular among families, but they don't detract from the scenic beauty for which the lake is best known.

Even if you're just passing through, take the short walk down to the water's edge and listen to the waves. The greenery around Big Lake is a soothing reminder of Mother Nature's ability to heal, and it's a fitting conclusion to a spectacular drive.

— *Noah Austin*

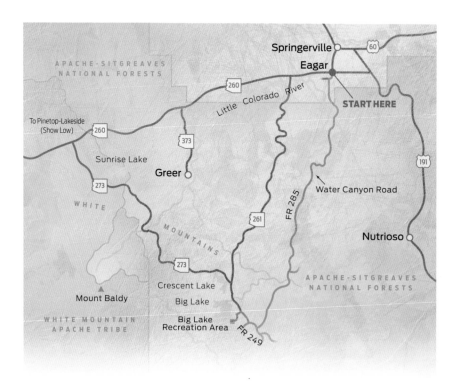

## TOUR GUIDE

**Note:** Mileages are approximate.

**Length:** 21 miles one way

**Directions:** From Show Low, go east on State Route 260 for 54 miles to Main Street in Eagar. Turn right onto Main Street and continue 1 mile to Forest Road 285 (Water Canyon Road). Turn left onto FR 285 and continue 18 miles to Forest Road 249. Turn right onto FR 249 and continue 2 miles to Big Lake Recreation Area, where FR 249 becomes State Route 273. To return to SR 260, either retrace your route or continue north on SR 273 to State Route 261, which intersects SR 260 near Eagar.

**Vehicle Requirements:** None

**Information:** Springerville Ranger District, 928-333-4301 or www.fs.usda.gov/asnf

# 25

# McNary to Vernon Loop

**A** crisp fall morning is the perfect time for this back-roads drive in the White Mountains. The 44.3-mile loop from McNary to Vernon begins and ends on White Mountain Apache Tribe land near Pinetop-Lakeside. It winds in and out of the Sitgreaves National Forest, through stands of pine and spruce interspersed with groves of aspen that make a spectacular fall display. A historic campground and a small, quiet lake make pleasant diversions along the way.

From Pinetop-Lakeside, we head east along State Route 260 about 8 miles to McNary. We pass the Apache Baptist Church, with its three plain white crosses, and turn left on Cady Avenue (County Road 3140). This becomes Vernon-McNary Road.

McNary was originally called Cluff Cienega, after a Mormon bishop who harvested hay for Fort Apache here in the late 19th century. Later renamed Cooley, it then became McNary after the McNary Lumber Co. bought the land in the 1920s. Today, McNary is a community of about 500 on tribal land.

The pavement ends in about a half-mile, and the road winds gently along a well-graded gravel route into the Sitgreaves National Forest. At 7 miles, we turn right at Forest Road 20 and drive the quarter-mile to Los Burros Campground.

Los Burros is a small, simple campground with a single picnic table and fire pit at each campsite, but the setting is beautiful. The campground sits at the edge of a grassy meadow, near the picturesque remains of a home, a barn and wooden corrals.

The buildings, with red board-and-bat siding and stone foundations, were built in 1909. A ranger once lived here and rode

Forest Road 224 passes through a stand of aspens and ponderosas on the route from McNary to Vernon.
NICK BEREZENKO

Near Los Burros Campground is an old house where a forest ranger once lived.
📷 PAUL GILL

a horse each day to Lake Mountain Lookout. The windows and doors of the house are boarded up, but viewing holes offer glimpses of the decaying interior.

The 13-mile Los Burros Trail begins at the campground and winds through a shady ponderosa-pine forest, and it includes a side trip to Lake Mountain Lookout. Mule deer and elk, as well as the occasional black bear, are often seen along the trail.

Back on Vernon-McNary Road, we head north. As we approach Vernon, the pines give way to juniper-dotted grasslands, and we begin to see homes scattered on the hillsides. Vernon was settled in the 1890s as a sawmill town. The area is now a growing bedroom community.

Finding no shops or restaurants in Vernon, we retrace our steps back down Vernon-McNary Road. Just past the Vernon cemetery, we turn left onto County Road 3261. It becomes Forest Road 61 as it re-enters the national forest, where pines reclaim the landscape. Many of the roads here are unmarked, so we are grateful that our GPS works, guiding us toward County Road 61 and Harris Lake.

After about 9 miles, we take a sharp left and drive the quarter-mile to a road on the right that leads down along the lake. The lake is very small, looking more like a wetland. But it's enough to attract wildlife, including a couple of reintroduced Mexican gray wolves that have been reported here. The lake is on private property, enclosed by a fence. But there is a meadow at the side of the road, which makes an agreeable place to picnic.

Backtracking our way along CR 61, we pick up Forest Road 96. This stretch is deeply rutted and rocky in places. But the forest is thicker and wilder here, with taller pines and more aspens. Some aspens appear quite old, with thick, scarred trunks.

In 8 miles, we're back to Vernon-McNary Road, where we turn left and drive back to McNary.

*— Kathy Montgomery*

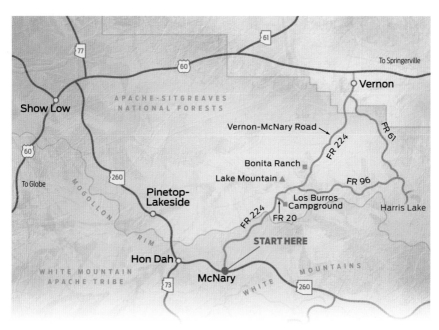

## TOUR GUIDE

**Note:** Mileages are approximate.

**Length:** 44.3-mile loop

**Directions:** From McNary, go north on Cady Avenue (County Road 3140), which becomes Vernon-McNary Road (Forest Road 224), for 7 miles to Forest Road 20, which leads to Los Burros Campground. Back on Vernon-McNary Road, continue another 10 miles to Vernon (the road will become CR 3140 again). Return south on Vernon-McNary Road. About 0.2 miles past the Vernon cemetery, turn left onto County Road 3261, which becomes Forest Road 61, and continue 2.4 miles to a "Y" intersection. Bear right onto Forest Road 404 (unmarked) and continue 1.2 miles to County Road 61 (also unmarked). Turn right onto CR 61 and continue 5 miles to a sharp left that leads to Harris Lake. Back on CR 61, backtrack north 1.5 miles to Forest Road 96. Turn left onto FR 96 and continue 8 miles back to Vernon-McNary Road. Turn left onto Vernon-McNary Road and continue 9 miles to State Route 260 at McNary.

**Vehicle requirements:** A high-clearance vehicle is required. Four-wheel-drive is recommended, particularly in wet conditions.

**Information:** Lakeside Ranger District, 928-368-2100 or www.fs.usda.gov/asnf

# 26

# Mogollon Rim Roads

Arizona has a lot of scenic beauty, but unless you count lakes, streams and the Colorado River on its western border, it lacks a coastline. However, get out of your car at any point along this 38-mile scenic drive on the Mogollon Rim, and you might start to wonder. If you close your eyes, you'll be hard-pressed to tell the difference between the sound of the wind whooshing through the ponderosas and the sound of waves crashing against some tropical beach.

Of course, it's not really a beach; it's a back road with rocks, and some of them are pretty sharp. That's why you'll want to take a four-wheel-drive vehicle and tread carefully and slowly. The sweeping panoramas you'll see atop the Mogollon Rim are worth the extra

On the Mogollon Rim, common sunflowers fill the void left by the devastating Rodeo-Chediski Fire.
📷 PAUL GILL

Black Canyon Lake is a popular fishing destination along the route.
PAUL GILL

time it might take you to get there.

The drive begins in Heber, and after you pass a few houses and businesses, you'll enter the Sitgreaves National Forest. A creek parallels the early part of the drive and crosses the road in a few places. It's there that you'll start seeing reminders of the Rodeo-Chediski Fire, the second-largest wildfire in Arizona's history. The fire burned more than 450,000 acres in the summer of 2002. There's plenty of living forest left to see here, but appreciate the burned-out areas for what they are: a reminder to put out campfires and dispose of cigarettes properly.

In addition to the scenery, the route features a number of informational markers. One of them, about 9 miles in, tells the story of Baca Meadow, a clearing where Juan and Damasia Baca built a home and raised eight children in the late 1800s. The meadow is also a great place to listen to the aforementioned wind through the ponderosas.

At Mile 12, you'll see a turnoff for Black Canyon Lake, a popular fishing spot. A few miles later, you'll find yourself on Forest Road 300, and at two points along it, you'll see stunning scenery on both sides of the road. The wildfire robbed this drive of a lot of trees, but it also opened up the canopy, and the views of forest to the north and south are spectacular.

Gentry Lookout, a wildfire watchtower, is located at Mile 18. There are picnic tables and grills there, so stop for lunch, say hello to the ranger on duty (if it's fire season) and enjoy another great view to the north. And don't leave the Rim without checking out the view to the south from the pullout at Mile 25. It's impressive.

Toward the end of this drive, you'll arrive at Phoenix Park, a large, lush meadow ringed by ponderosas and other evergreens. Look for a sandstone chimney that marks where an old ranch building once stood. From there, it's just another few miles to the end of the drive — 10 miles east of where you started, and even farther from the beach.

*— Noah Austin*

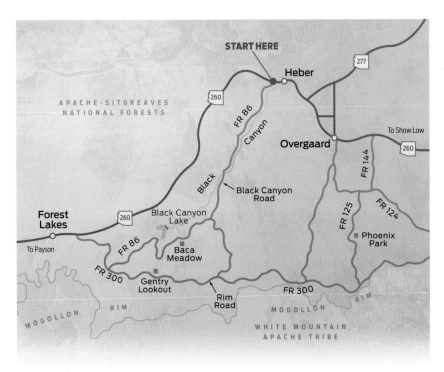

## TOUR GUIDE

**Note:** Mileages are approximate.

**Length:** 38 miles one way

**Directions:** From Payson, go east on State Route 260 for 51 miles to Black Canyon Lane. Turn right onto Black Canyon Lane, a dirt road that soon turns into Black Canyon Road (Forest Road 86), and continue 15.3 miles to Forest Road 300. Turn left onto FR 300 and continue 14.3 miles to Forest Road 125. Turn left onto FR 125 and continue 4.9 miles to Forest Road 124. Turn right onto FR 124 and continue a half-mile to Forest Road 144. Turn left onto FR 144 and continue 3 miles back to SR 260 near Overgaard.

**Vehicle requirements:** A high-clearance, four-wheel-drive vehicle is required. This drive is not recommended in inclement weather.

**Information:** Black Mesa Ranger District, 928-535-7300 or www.fs.usda.gov/asnf

# 27

# Young Highway

**T**he first thing you need to know about this National Scenic Byway — officially known as the Desert to Tall Pines Scenic Road but informally known as the Young Highway — is that it isn't a drive you can do before lunchtime. This 74-mile back road, from State Route 260 near Payson to State Route 188 north of Globe, winds through ponderosa pines and grasslands before shifting abruptly to the saguaros of Arizona's high desert. Large sections of the road are unpaved or lack guardrails, so patience — along with a light foot on the accelerator — is a must. Pack a picnic lunch, and take your time. The scenery, particularly toward the end, is worth it.

Heading south on Forest Road 512, past an aspen grove, you'll come to the first of two areas hit by recent wildfires. Despite the devastation, you'll see that saplings are springing up to replace the burned ponderosas. A little farther south, as you crest a hill at Mile 14, you'll get a nice look at the Mogollon Rim on your right. It's the first of many breathtaking views. Several pullouts line this narrow road, so stop frequently and enjoy the panoramas — particularly at Mile 19 — that show the stark contrast between the wildfire-scorched trees on the left and the dense forest on the right.

From there, you'll descend into Young, an isolated community that didn't even have

Fog shrouds the distant Roosevelt Lake, as seen from the red-rock cliffs along the Young Highway.
📷 RANDY PRENTICE

The snow-covered Four Peaks are visible from State Route 288 south of Young.
📷 RANDY PRENTICE

outside electricity until the mid-1960s. Fewer than 700 people call Young home, and a drive through it is like traveling back in time. It's a good place to stop for lunch, either the one you packed or the one you'll order at Antlers, the town's only restaurant.

South of Young, the road climbs again, and a vista point at Mile 31 provides another view of the Mogollon Rim, along with the town below. The canopy then begins to open up as small trees and bushes replace the taller pines, and on a clear day, the blue sky, combined with the silence of this isolated area, is spectacular.

At Mile 41, McFadden Peak (7,135 feet above sea level) dominates the view as you begin the descent into the desert. You'll pass several lush riparian areas, and the streams offer excellent opportunities to see birds, deer and other wildlife. But the real payoff is an incredible panorama of Roosevelt Lake, with its surrounding red cliffs and mountains to the south. The jaw-dropping views continue for several miles, but be careful not to let them lead you off the road — there are numerous sharp turns as you lose altitude.

Before long, you'll find yourself among the saguaros and prickly pear cactuses that are the Sonoran Desert's trademarks. Once you've dropped into the desert, it's just a short drive to a one-lane bridge over the Salt River, and another short trip from there to the drive's conclusion at State Route 188. After the leisurely pace that's necessary on the Young Highway, the trip back home will feel like light speed by comparison.

— *Noah Austin*

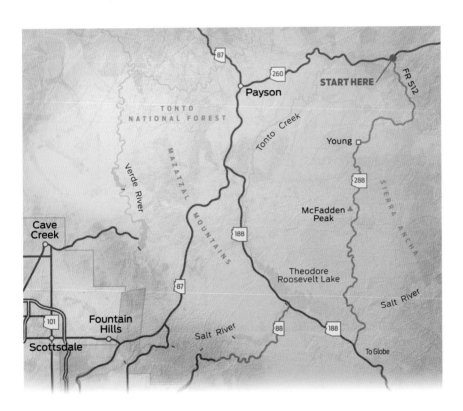

## TOUR GUIDE

**Note:** Mileages are approximate.

**Length:** 74 miles one way

**Directions:** From Payson, go east on State Route 260 for 32 miles to Forest Road 512. Turn right onto FR 512, which turns into State Route 288 (Young Highway), and continue 74 miles to State Route 188 near Globe.

**Vehicle requirements:** A standard SUV is recommended. While the road is passable with a sedan in good weather, some mountainous sections receive little sunlight and might remain muddy or icy for several days after a storm.

**Information:** Pleasant Valley Ranger District, 928-462-4300 or www.fs.usda.gov/tonto

# WESTERN
# ARIZONA

Sunset light bathes willow and tamarisk trees along the shore of Lake Mohave.
📷 DEREK VON BRIESEN

# 28

# Cottonwood Road

There are plenty of reasons to enjoy the 19-mile-long Cottonwood Road, which begins at U.S. Route 93, between Kingman and Hoover Dam, and ends at serene Lake Mohave. Maybe you're on your way to Las Vegas for the weekend and you'd like a little peace and quiet before you hit the casino floor. Or maybe you're on your way back from a weekend in Vegas, your foolproof roulette strategy ("Put it all on 36; I've got a feeling about that number") having left you without money for a hotel room, and you're looking for a place to camp. Either way, you'll find what you need on this drive, but it doesn't have to be a Sin City side trip. As you'll see,

Willow trees are reflected in the calm water of Lake Mohave, the payoff to a sometimes-rugged drive on Cottonwood Road.
📷 DEREK VON BRIESEN

The rugged Black Mountains loom over the Arizona side of Lake Mohave.
📷 DEREK VON BRIESEN

Cottonwood Road is a safe bet almost anytime.

To begin, reset your odometer when you turn onto Cottonwood Road from U.S. 93. The entire road is dirt, but the western half is smooth and well-traveled. Yuccas and other high-desert vegetation are the norm here, and this is farm country, so don't be surprised to also see a herd of cows or goats (yes, goats) ambling across the road. Soon, on your right, you'll pass Mount Perkins (5,456 feet), and then you'll begin a gradual climb into the Black Mountains, which parallel Arizona's western border with Nevada. The mountains might not look like much from the east, but ... well, just wait.

Around Mile 10, the terrain shifts abruptly and the road follows suit. It's much more rough and washboard-like from here on in, and you'll be glad you've got four-wheel-drive. After an initial uphill section, the road slopes downward as you descend toward Lake Mohave. Your first great view of the lake comes at Mile 13.

A half-mile from the lake, you'll reach a fork. For the best view, go left to stay on Cottonwood Road. Before long, you'll come to a lakeside clearing with restrooms and a few primitive campsites. The clearing is mostly surrounded by wetland vegetation, and don't be surprised to see a turkey vulture or two hanging out in a nearby tree. Like all vultures, they're mostly scavengers, so they're probably waiting around to see whether you're going to drop dead. Don't take it personally.

If you don't plan to spend the night, at least spend a few minutes taking in the scenery. To the west, on the Nevada side of Lake Mohave, are the Eldorado and Newberry mountains and Cottonwood Cove Marina. To the east — that is, behind you — the Black Mountains appear much more impressive from this lower vantage point. From its shores, it's easy to see why Lake Mohave is a popular recreation spot. If you do plan to stay, there's a 14-day camping limit. But that should be more than enough time to get over a rough weekend in Vegas.

— *Noah Austin*

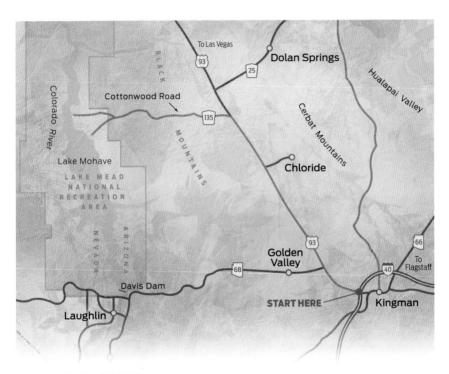

## TOUR GUIDE

**Note:** Mileages are approximate.

**Length:** 19 miles one way

**Directions:** From the intersection of Interstate 40 and U.S. Route 93 in Kingman, go north on U.S. 93 for 25.5 miles to Cottonwood Road. Turn left onto Cottonwood Road and continue 19 miles to Lake Mohave. Retrace your steps to return to Kingman, or continue north on U.S. 93 to reach Hoover Dam and Las Vegas.

**Vehicle requirements:** A four-wheel-drive vehicle is required. Cottonwood Road crosses several washes; don't enter them when they're flooded.

**Information:** Lake Mead National Recreation Area, 702-293-8906 or www.nps.gov/lake

# 29

# Kingman to Pearce Ferry

I t's indisputable (in the opinion of one *Arizona Highways* writer, anyway) that *I Still Haven't Found What I'm Looking For* is the best song U2 ever made. And maybe Bono and his buddies had a route like the one to Pearce Ferry — near the eastern bank of Lake Mead — in mind when they recorded 1987's *The Joshua Tree*, where that song is found. You'll climb a few mountains and run through some fields on this drive, but the real stars of the show are the Joshua trees. And there are a lot of them.

Your drive begins on Stockton Hill Road in Kingman, a place whose small-town charm is worth a stop the next time you pass through on Interstate 40. Heading north, you'll leave the city, but not before seeing the road's namesake, Stockton Hill (5,938 feet), on your left. Soon, you'll enter the Hualapai Valley, and it's here that *Yucca brevifolia* makes its first appearance. Joshua trees are one of the species predicted to be

The Lake Mead area is the payoff to the 69-mile drive from Kingman to Pearce Ferry.
📷 RANDY PRENTICE

Joshua trees, one of Nature's strangest-looking plants, crowd the landscape along Stockton Hill Road and Pierce Ferry Road.
📷 RANDY PRENTICE

most imperiled by climate change, but you wouldn't know it on this drive: There are vast swaths of the odd-looking plants, and in some places, they're so densely packed that their limbs almost touch.

The Hualapai Valley is flanked by two mountain ranges that couldn't be more different. To the west are the Cerbat Mountains, a rocky range that's home to a herd of wild horses. To the east are the Grand Wash Cliffs, which bear a striking resemblance to the cliffs and buttes of the nearby Grand Canyon. There's more of that to come, so keep heading north until you reach Pierce Ferry Road, which is spelled differently than Pearce Ferry, the ultimate destination. Then, hang a right.

The Joshua trees get even thicker as you continue, and you'll soon reach Diamond Bar Road. This road leads to the Grand Canyon Skywalk, a tourist attraction on Hualapai Tribe land. Today, though, continue on Pierce Ferry Road. The road leads into Lake Mead National Recreation Area, where the Joshua trees begin to thin as the moonscape of the Lake Mead area takes over.

The final 5 miles are the only unpaved portion of this drive, but the dirt road is well maintained and smooth. It's also dusty, so keep your distance if there's another vehicle in front of you. You'll know you've reached Pearce Ferry when you see a picnic area and restrooms on your right. You'll also find information on the history of the area. Pearce Ferry once was a popular destination for Hoover Dam tourists, and in the 1930s and '40s, there were plans to build a resort there.

Today, there isn't much left. But that's OK. The scenery — Grand Canyon cliffs to the east and Lake Mead mountains to the west — is a worthy payoff after a 69-mile journey. It's where you'll find what you were looking for.

— *Noah Austin*

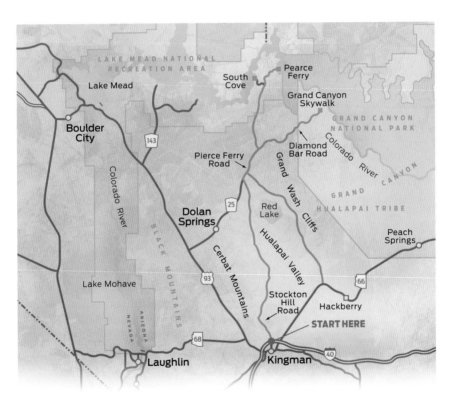

## TOUR GUIDE

**Note:** Mileages are approximate.

**Length:** 69 miles one way

**Directions:** From the intersection of Interstate 40 and Stockton Hill Road in Kingman, go north on Stockton Hill Road for 41.5 miles to Pierce Ferry Road. Turn right onto Pierce Ferry Road and continue 27.5 miles to Pearce Ferry.

**Vehicle requirements:** None, but avoid Stockton Hill Road if rain is expected. The road crosses several washes, and you should not enter them if they're flooded.

**Information:** Lake Mead National Recreation Area, 702-293-8906 or www.nps.gov/lake

## 30

# Red Cloud Mine Road

**D**epending on which poll you believe, 5 to 10 percent of Americans think the Apollo moon landings were a hoax. That observation might seem like an odd lede for a scenic drive, but as you head up Red Cloud Mine Road in the Imperial National Wildlife Refuge, north of Yuma, the reference makes more sense. The views along this rugged, isolated back road are a different kind of scenic: There's almost no vegetation, and the rocky buttes could easily pass for a moonscape with a little 1960s-era color correction.

It's enough to get the gears turning in any conspiracy theorist's head, and the fact that the route passes through a U.S. Army proving ground might make you wonder whether there's something here that someone doesn't want you to see.

Or, if you're among the other 90 to 95 percent of the country, you could just enjoy this 16-mile drive, which starts at Martinez Lake, a popular destination for birders, photographers and anglers. The lake was formed in 1935, when Imperial Dam, on the Colorado River, was completed. About a mile in, you'll get a good view of the lake — the greenery surrounding it is a striking contrast with the surrounding desert.

Red Cloud Mine Road cuts through a tamarisk forest near the Trigo Mountains Wilderness.
📷 RANDY PRENTICE

Mounds of multicolored sediment highlight the second half of the drive on Red Cloud Mine Road.
📷 RANDY PRENTICE

After that, the road narrows and gets rougher, so take your time around corners and over medium-sized rocks. You'll be hard-pressed to find cellphone service out here, and even in January, this isn't a place you want to have car trouble. At Mile 5, you'll pass the trailhead for the Painted Desert Trail, one of two designated hiking trails in the refuge.

Shortly after that, the colors that give that trail its name — red, pink, yellow, black and several shades of brown — will begin to show themselves on the surrounding buttes. Once you enter the Army's Yuma Proving Ground at Mile 7, you'll start seeing signs warning you to avoid "unexploded ordnance." It's perfectly safe to pull over and make a few pictures, but don't stray off the roadway.

Fourteen miles in, you'll come upon perhaps the best views of the drive. Colorful buttes are everywhere as you descend into a small valley — you're likely to see a hawk or two circling above. Just beyond there, you'll see a small mining facility on your left. It's the only significant sign of civilization on this route, and because Red Cloud Mine Road isn't maintained beyond this point, it's a good place to stop awhile before retracing your route back to Martinez Lake.

The alternative is to take along an all-terrain vehicle and continue north. If you do that, you'll eventually end up in Cibola National Wildlife Refuge, which straddles the Arizona-California border. You could probably get there in a lunar rover, too. And who knows? There might be one from the Apollo missions stashed somewhere along the road.

*— Noah Austin*

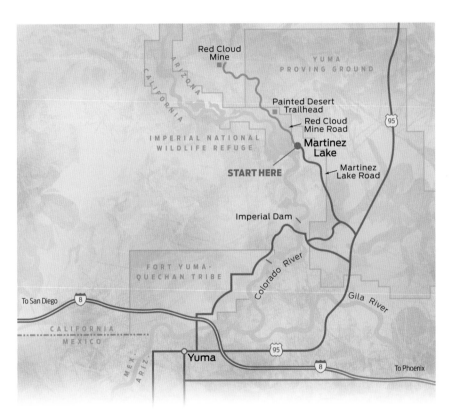

## TOUR GUIDE

**Note:** Mileages are approximate.

**Length:** 16 miles one way

**Directions:** From Yuma, go north on U.S. Route 95 for 24 miles to Martinez Lake Road. Turn left onto Martinez Lake Road and continue 10 miles to Red Cloud Mine Road. Turn right onto Red Cloud Mine Road and continue 16 miles before retracing your route back to Yuma.

**Vehicle requirements:** A high-clearance, four-wheel-drive vehicle is required.

**Information:** Imperial National Wildlife Refuge, 928-783-3371 or www.fws.gov/southwest/refuges

# 31

# Six Mile Crossing

**T**here are times when the roads that lead to a scenic drive are anything but scenic. And some roads seem endless, even boring. "Are we there yet?" becomes the mantra of those stuck in the car. Yet you drive on because the payoff — endless vistas of stunning Arizona wilderness — is worth it. The drive to Six Mile Crossing has a definite payoff, but the scenery along the way is impressive, too. This trip is all about beautiful landscapes, from start to finish.

To reach Burro Creek Crossing Road, which is the link to Six Mile Crossing, travel north from Wickenburg on U.S. Route 93. It isn't far into the drive before the landscape is suddenly covered in Joshua trees.

Designated the Joshua Tree Parkway of Arizona, this 54-mile stretch of U.S. 93 is spectacular, and because the road winds and climbs, you're guaranteed several excellent views of these beautiful,

Saguaros are among the scenery along Burro Creek Crossing Road on the way to Six Mile Crossing.
RICK GIASE

Intertwining ocotillos reach skyward in front of a butte near Six Mile Crossing.
📷 RICK GIASE

bizarre-looking plants. If Mother Nature is kind and the right amount of rain falls at the right time of year, clusters of white-green blossoms sprout from the tips of the *Yucca brevifolia* in the spring.

As the signs for Burro Creek begin to appear, start paying attention to the milepost numbers. The turnoff to Burro Creek Crossing Road is around Milepost 132. Keep in mind there isn't a turning lane, so you'll want to slow down as you approach, and make sure you use your turn signal to give the folks behind you a heads-up. Once you make the turn, you'll see a sign that reads: "Primitive Road. Caution. Use at Your Own Risk." In spite of the warning, Burro Creek Crossing Road is a well-maintained, graded dirt road that can be navigated with a sedan, weather permitting.

Heading east, saguaros, chollas and ocotillos replace the Joshua trees, and it isn't long before you're treated to some very nice views of Arizona's backcountry. Although you'll be less than a mile from the heavily traveled U.S. 93, you'll feel a world away — other than the piles of scat, a few cattle crossings and tire tracks, it's just you and Mother Nature. That said, take it slow and be mindful of the occasional oncoming vehicle. For the next 7.5 miles, the road narrows as you climb the hillside. And then, at Mile 5.3, the road becomes rough, but it's temporary. A flash-flood sign serves as a reminder to skip this drive during inclement weather.

Around Mile 8, you'll see the tailings dam from the Freeport-McMoRan

Copper & Gold Mine. It's an unexpected and unnatural scar on Mother Nature's otherwise pristine canvas. As the road begins to descend in a series of switchbacks, the scenery shifts once again as cottonwood trees erupt from the ground, their leaves providing shade as you bump along toward Burro Creek.

The creek is a lush, life-giving stream for the javelinas, toads, mosquitofish and raptors that inhabit the area. It's also the payoff of this scenic drive. Beauty certainly abounds en route, but it's here, as you walk along the banks of the creek, that you'll want to thank Mother Nature for her impressive handiwork.

— *Kathy Ritchie*

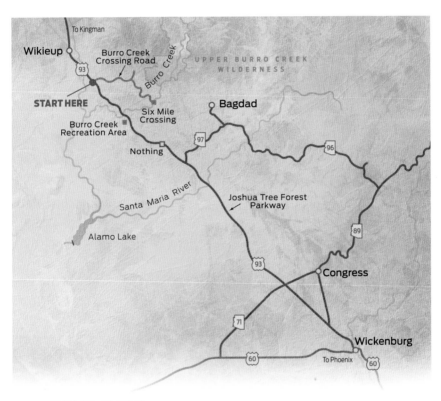

## TOUR GUIDE

**Note:** Mileages are approximate.

**Length:** 14.5 miles one way

**Directions:** From Wickenburg, go north on U.S. Route 93 for 65 miles to Burro Creek Crossing Road (Milepost 132). Turn right onto Burro Creek Crossing Road and continue 14.5 miles to Six Mile Crossing. Retrace your route to return to U.S. 93.

**Vehicle requirements:** A high-clearance vehicle is recommended. Do not cross Burro Creek unless you have a four-wheel-drive vehicle.

**Information:** Bureau of Land Management, Kingman Field Office, 928-718-3700 or www.blm.gov/az

Looking east, sprawling grasslands define the scenery along Empire Ranch Road.
📷 JOHN SHERMAN

# SOUTHERN ARIZONA

# 32

# Box Canyon Road

**T**he Melendrez Fire was started by lightning. Not a cigarette butt. It's an important distinction. One source, of course, is natural; the other is not. In either case, the effects of fire can be devastating. But not always. As you make your way along Box Canyon Road, you'll see that in some cases, when fire is allowed to run its natural course, it can make an already scenic drive even more beautiful. This is one of those cases.

Although Box Canyon Road comes with a lesson in fire management and ecology, it still meets our prerequisite of being scenic. The all-dirt road begins about 3 miles north of the entrance to Madera Canyon, which ranks as one of the most spectacular places in Arizona. Among other things, the canyon features four life zones and is home to more than 250 species of birds — even if you lean more toward Miss America than Miss Hathaway, you'll be impressed. Make time if you can. If not, the road awaits.

Heading east, the 14-mile route (washboard all the way) parallels the north side of the Santa Rita Mountains. Almost immediately, you'll see the effects of the fire, which burned more than 5,800

The multicolored vegetation on the hills of Box Canyon offers a lesson in fire management and ecology.
📷 RANDY PRENTICE

Yellow wildflowers flourish in the grasslands beneath the Santa Rita Mountains.
📷 RANDY PRENTICE

acres in May 2009. In particular, you'll see a sea of green in the summer. According to Heidi Schewel of the Coronado National Forest, the fire burned at a low intensity, which was very good for the landscape.

"There was little tree mortality," she says, "and the dried grass and brush was burned off. The resulting ash will act as a natural fertilizer. Remember Science 101 and photosynthesis? Living plants take in moisture from the roots and carbon dioxide through their leaves, and use sunlight and chlorophyll to produce energy. This energy is locked up in the biomass. When a fire of this sort burns through, those nutrients are returned to the soil and made available. Add a little rain, and the grasses will flourish."

The sea of green notwithstanding, it's the mountains that stand out most on this scenic drive. The Santa Ritas are an impressive range, with plenty of oaks and cottonwoods, so if you make the drive in fall, you should see some color if you look to your right. To your left, the views will include the road's namesake, as well as open grasslands and impressive groves of enormous ocotillos.

After about 5 miles, you'll leave the Santa Rita Experimental Range (a project of the agriculture department at the University of Arizona) and enter the Coronado National Forest. The road along this stretch is narrow, winding and without any guardrails. Go slowly, and plan on stopping for photos. Eventually, after about 10 miles, the road reaches the top of its climb, where the views are dominated by grasslands that stretch as far as the eye can see. It's vintage Southern Arizona.

The road ends a few miles later at its intersection with State Route 83, just north of Sonoita. At this point, most people continue north toward Tucson, while some head south to grab a bite in Sonoita. Either way, it's an opportunity to think about where you've been, and how fire, when orchestrated by Mother Nature, can make an already scenic drive even more beautiful.

— *Robert Stieve*

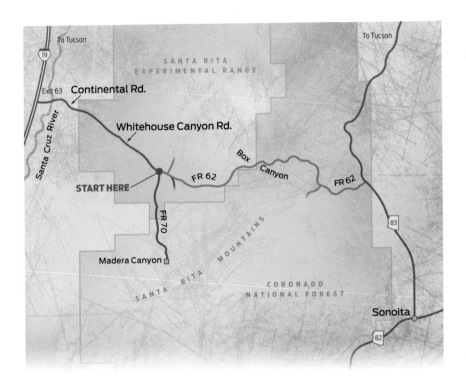

## TOUR GUIDE

**Note:** Mileages are approximate.

**Length:** 14 miles one way

**Directions:** From Tucson, go south on Interstate 19 for 24 miles to Continental Road (Exit 63). Turn left (east) onto Continental Road and continue 1 mile to Whitehouse Canyon Road (look for the signs to Madera Canyon). Turn right onto Whitehouse Canyon Road and continue 7.3 miles to the intersection of Forest Road 62 and Forest Road 70. Veer left onto FR 62 and continue 14 miles to State Route 83.

**Vehicle requirements:** None

**Information:** Nogales Ranger District, 520-281-2296 or www.fs.usda.gov/coronado

# 33

# Empire Ranch Road

It's hard to believe that Las Cienegas National Conservation Area was, at one time, at risk of becoming a master-planned community and golf course. Instead, the locals rallied, and in 1986, the area came under the protection of the Bureau of Land Management. In 1988, it became part of the National Landscape Conservation System. Today, it's accessed by a 24-mile drive that's best described as spectacular.

But before you head out, be warned: Although the landscape, with its rolling grasslands and verdant riparian area, is magnificent, the road itself isn't. It's challenging at times and might require four-wheel-drive in places.

A Bureau of Land Management road near Empire Ranch meanders through rolling grasslands and mesquite trees.
📷 RANDY PRENTICE

Willows thrive in the lush riparian area near Cienega Creek along Empire Ranch Road.
📷 RANDY PRENTICE

To begin, turn left off of State Route 83 onto the gravel road marked "Historic Empire Ranch" and continue for 3 miles to a "T" junction. There, turn left onto Bureau of Land Management Road 6901 and follow the sign to Oak Tree Canyon. Some area maps list the route as Bureau of Land Management Road 901, but the agency updated its signage to include a numerical prefix that indicates road condition. In this case, the "6" means "off road." Moving along, you'll quickly come to the riparian area around Empire Gulch. At about Mile 4, the cottonwood trees and mesquite bosque lining the road give way to vast open grasslands. Just beyond the rolling hills, you'll enter another riparian area, where you'll cross Cienega Creek. As you pass over a bridge, a small sea of cattails hides any sign of water, but the reeds are beautiful and unexpected. Around Mile 8, the road turns left, then abruptly right. At that point, you'll be on Bureau of Land Management Road 6914.

This is where you can expect a few challenging conditions. That's because the road is maintained on an as-needed basis. Besides a few bumps in the road, you'll also cross several sandy washes (don't even think about attempting them in inclement weather). In addition, the conservation area hosts a working ranch, so you might encounter a few cows. Thus, it's important to leave gates as you find them. Pronghorns, mule deer and bobcats are also prevalent in the area, as are black-tailed prairie dogs, which the Arizona Game and Fish Department reintroduced to the area in 2008 and 2009.

Near Mile 11, you'll begin a serious climb, but the payoff is a spectacular view of the Whetstone Mountains on your left. As soon as you reach the top, the road drops, and for the next mile or so, it becomes increasingly difficult to navigate. Take your time. If you can safely transition into four-wheel-drive, do so, because the narrow road twists and turns sharply.

As the road begins to level out, you'll face another potential obstacle: a fork in the road, where there are no clear markers to indicate which road is BLM 6914. Continue in the direction you were already headed — southwest. At Mile 13.9, you'll cross another sandy wash, and in less than 1.5 miles, the road connects with Bureau of Land Management Road 6900. This marks the final stages of the drive, and by Mile 24, you should be back where you started.

*— Kathy Ritchie*

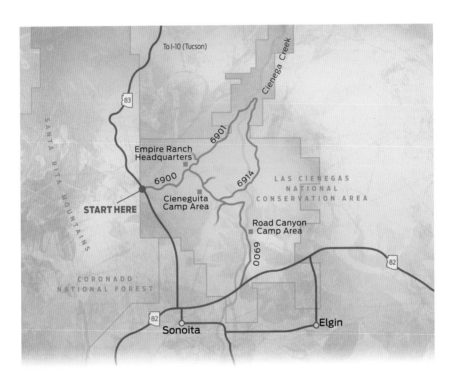

## TOUR GUIDE

**Note:** Mileages are approximate.

**Length:** 24 miles round-trip (from State Route 83)

**Directions:** From Tucson, go east on Interstate 10 for 23 miles to State Route 83. Turn right onto SR 83 and continue 19 miles to Historic Empire Ranch Road (Bureau of Land Management Road 6900). Turn left onto Historic Empire Ranch Road and continue 3 miles to Bureau of Land Management Road 6901. Turn left onto BLM 6901 and continue 8.4 miles to Bureau of Land Management Road 6914. Turn right onto BLM 6914 and continue 7 miles to BLM 6900. Turn right onto BLM 6900 and continue 5.6 miles until you arrive at the starting point of the drive.

**Vehicle requirements:** A high-clearance, four-wheel-drive vehicle is required.

**Information:** Las Cienegas National Conservation Area, 520-439-6400 or www.blm.gov/az

# 34

# Geronimo Trail

The Geronimo Trail in Southern Arizona feels as remote as just about any drive in Arizona. But it wasn't always that way. The route once was a major migration corridor for Apache Indians, as well as Spanish explorers, missionaries, Mormons and Mexican revolutionaries, just to name a few.

Today, the Geronimo Trail offers scenery, solitude and a good bit of history along the U.S.-Mexico border. The entire stretch extends nearly 80 miles from Douglas, Arizona, to Animas, New Mexico. For this trip, we turned back at a historical marker about 37 miles east of Douglas, just past the New Mexico border.

East 15th Street in Douglas becomes the Geronimo Trail at its intersection with West Airport Road. Heading east out of town, the pavement gives way to a wide gravel road after about 4 miles.

Beyond the gentle rise of the Perilla Mountains on the outskirts of Douglas, most of the drive is through broad, flat San Bernardino Valley, with the Peloncillo Mountains visible in the distance. Pronghorns inhabit the grasslands north of the trail.

Agave stalks reach skyward near sunset in the Peloncillo Mountains along the Geronimo Trail.
RANDY PRENTICE

Granite formations contrast with cottonwood and sycamore trees on the Geronimo Trail.
📷 RANDY PRENTICE

About 14 miles from Douglas, you'll find the turnoff to Slaughter Ranch, officially the San Bernardino Ranch National Historic Landmark.

Father Eusebio Kino is believed to have passed through here in 1694 during one of his expeditions. Captain Juan Bautista de Anza, who founded San Francisco, headquartered here in 1773. The ranch itself dates to an 1846 Mexican land grant. Ignacio Perez bought the original 73,240 acres for 90 pesos but was soon run off by Apaches.

"Texas" John Slaughter bought 65,000 acres of the original grant in 1884. It was mostly wetlands at the time, and the Gadsden Purchase had redrawn the U.S.-Mexico border right through the property. Slaughter later retired to the ranch after two terms as Cochise County sheriff.

The Johnson Historical Museum of the Southwest and the U.S. Fish and Wildlife Service bought the homesite in the early 1980s. The museum took 131 acres and restored the historic buildings, which opened to the public in 1985. An adjacent 2,300 acres became the San Bernardino National Wildlife Refuge.

History buffs can tour the buildings and explore the nearby ruins of a military outpost meant to protect the Slaughter family from Pancho Villa during the Mexican Revolution.

But you'll want to spend some time near the spring-fed lake Slaughter built. Willows and cottonwoods surround the lake, shimmering gold in the fall. Pied-billed grebes dive into the water while vermilion flycatchers make their brilliant display in the trees above. It's a magical place, and you can easily spend the day.

Back on the Geronimo Trail, the volcanic rock and yellow grasses flanking the road make the lushness of Slaughter Ranch feel like a mirage. But at the foothills of the Peloncillo Mountains, the landscape begins to change. The twisty road follows a creek bed lined with sycamores. As it gains elevation, oaks and junipers give way to dramatic rock formations.

The New Mexico border lies about 3 miles past the entrance to the Coronado National Forest. As the crow flies, it's not far from where Geronimo surrendered to U.S. troops in 1886. We press on a little farther to Clanton Draw, where a historical marker memorializes the Mormon Battalion, which crossed in 1846, lowering its wagons down the 40 percent grade with ropes.

Contemplating the hardships of that journey makes the 37-mile drive back to Douglas feel like the luxury it is.

— *Kathy Montgomery*

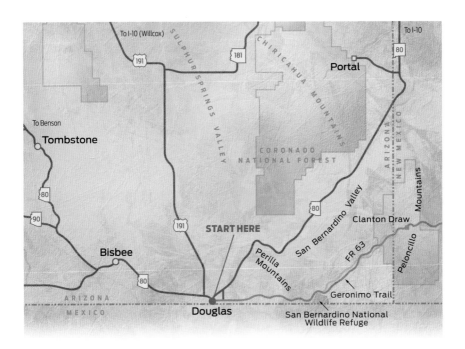

## TOUR GUIDE

**Note:** Mileages are approximate.

**Length:** 37 miles one way (Douglas to Clanton Draw)

**Directions:** From Douglas, go east on 15th Street, which turns into Geronimo Trail (Forest Road 63), for 37 miles to Clanton Draw, just past the Arizona-New Mexico border.

**Vehicle requirements:** A high-clearance, four-wheel-drive vehicle is recommended. but the road is passable in a sedan in good weather.

**Information:** John Slaughter Ranch and Museum, 520-678-7935 or www.slaughterranch.com; Douglas Ranger District, 520-364-3468 or www.fs.usda.gov/coronado

# 35

# Mescal Road

**T**ucson is one big city — not as big as Phoenix and nowhere near as big as L.A., but big enough. That's why it's so surprising that Mescal Road, a nearly 16-mile stretch of scenic byway, is so close to the city limits. Literally, it's just over the creek and through the woods.

The drive begins on Mescal Road, about 40 miles east of Tucson, off of Interstate 10 at Exit 297, and meanders past a few small private properties before opening onto fields of yucca and fragrant creosote. After approximately 2 miles, the paved road crosses a set of railroad tracks, then becomes rockier as it approaches an Old West town after another mile. It's not a real town, just a replica that Old Tucson Studios used as a set for the last few episodes of *Bonanza* and for movies such as *The Quick and the Dead*. Although the set is closed to the public and visitors are forbidden from approaching for a closer look, it's easy to use your imagination and picture gunfights and sarsaparilla-slinging.

Beyond the movie set, the pavement ends, but the road is still passable in a

The Miller Creek Trail, which starts at the end of Mescal Road, offers incredible views of the Rincon Mountains.
📷 ELIAS BUTLER

The road crosses Paige Creek, which flows across granite boulders dotted with Indian paintbrushes.
📷 JACK DYKINGA

standard-clearance vehicle. As it continues, the creosote thins to make way for thick stands of wild grasses, particularly as the road becomes hillier at approximately 4.7 miles. Later, cottonwoods, sycamores and manzanitas will become visual staples.

Five miles in, you'll encounter your first water crossing — one of many, as the road traverses both Ash and Paige creeks. Here, the city seems more distant than it is, and the road continues past a cattle pen — where the cows are more than happy to oblige a photo opportunity with moos and cud-chewing — and Ash Canyon Ranch.

Past the ranch, the road is at its rockiest and, in fact, its steepest. It tops out at Mile 7 and becomes smooth again. After another mile, it's possible to pull into a rustic campsite, where a downed tree provides the perfect perch for a picnic. Sadly, you might discover the remnants of someone else's party, as some visitors find this an appropriate place to bid farewell to their garbage. On a happier note, you might also happen upon a horse that's wandered from the nearby B&D Ranch. Or maybe some deer.

Just beyond the halfway point, it's possible to be in two places at one time. At nearly 9 miles down the road, you'll straddle the line between Cochise and Pima counties, where stands of ocotillos appear along the roadside like cryptic fingers emerging from the boulder-strewn soil. From there, the road becomes — in parts — patchy and occasionally turbulent, but remains passable.

After another 3 miles, the road once again climbs, this time up a hill that provides a spectacular view of the Little Rincon and Galiuro mountains, as well as Happy Valley. At the bottom of the hill, the road cuts through a grassy pasture and past several ranch properties. One-tenth of a mile beyond the pasture, you'll see a sign for the Miller Creek Trailhead. The path, which is part of the Arizona Trail, winds to the edge of Saguaro National Park. There, the road ends, but another great picnic spot lies just a few hundred feet from the trailhead.

— *Kelly Vaughn Kramer*

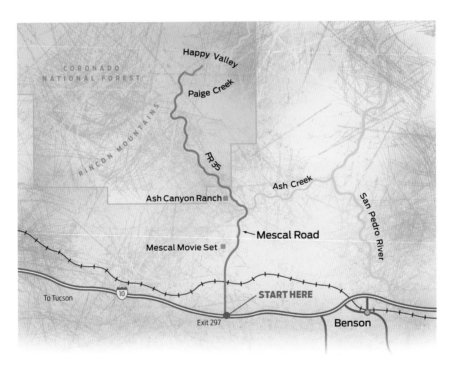

## TOUR GUIDE

**Note:** Mileages are approximate.
**Length:** 16 miles one way
**Directions:** From Tucson, go east on Interstate 10 for 32 miles to Mescal Road (Exit 297). Turn left onto Mescal Road and continue 16 miles to the Miller Creek Trailhead.
**Vehicle requirements:** None
**Information:** Santa Catalina Ranger District, 520-749-8700 or www.fs.usda.gov/coronado

# 36

# Catalina Highway

As *Arizona Highways* contributor Craig Childs will tell you, going from the Colorado River to the rim of the Grand Canyon is the ecological equivalent of walking from Mexico to Canada in less than 10 miles. Plants, animals, weather ... they all change dramatically as you gain elevation. There's no journey like it on Earth. But you can't do the Canyon in a car.

Down south, however, there is a vehicle-friendly version of this ascension through the ecosystems. The Catalina Highway, also known as the Sky Island Scenic Byway, climbs Mount Lemmon, the highest peak of the

The setting sun lights a rock formation near Windy Point Vista along the Catalina Highway.
📷 RANDY PRENTICE

The road winds through several plant communities as it climbs Mount Lemmon.
📷 RANDY PRENTICE

Santa Catalina Mountains. You won't get all the way to the 9,100-foot summit on this drive, but don't be surprised if the temperature at the end is 30 degrees lower than when you got into your car.

The 30-mile drive begins at Tanque Verde Road in Tucson, and the first few miles are mostly flat. The desert vegetation at the outset is typical of the Sonoran Desert, but once you begin the climb, you'll see hillsides crammed with saguaros, which appear taller and thinner than those along, say, Interstate 17 north of Phoenix. It's likely that some of them have been on these hills for 150 years or longer. But before you've had time to really ponder that, the saguaros give way to scrub bushes as the road heads uphill.

Numerous pullouts and vista points line the route up the mountain. They're all beautiful and worth a look, but if you're in a hurry, there are two in particular you'll want to hit. The first is Windy Point, about 18 miles into the drive. The view of the Tucson area is spectacular, and it's easy to see why this vista is a popular wedding spot. Just beyond that point, near a sign marking an elevation of 7,000 feet, you'll see your first ponderosa pine. Those tall trees become the dominant vegetation for the next several miles.

Before long, aspens start appearing along the road, and at Mile 27, you'll see a stunning panorama on the right. Aspen Vista Point, the other can't-miss stop on the drive, offers the first great look to the north. An interpretive sign here spells out the wonder of this drive: From start to finish, you're passing through six vegetation communities, starting with the Sonoran Desert and ending with a mixed-conifer forest. In between is a mix of grassland, woodland and forest.

From Aspen Vista, it's only a few more miles to Summerhaven, which marks the end of this drive. Although the Aspen Fire of 2003 burned a portion of the village, the community is as vibrant as ever. When you're there, stop by the Cookie Cabin for dinner or dessert. And enjoy the cooler weather. Even in September, you might need a sweater.

*— Noah Austin*

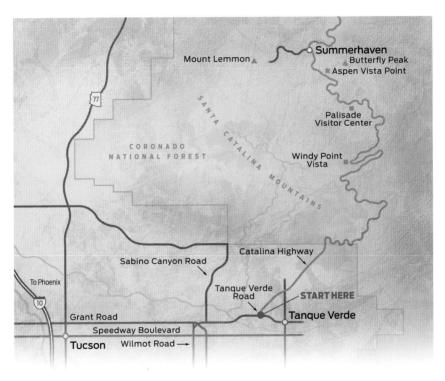

## TOUR GUIDE

**Note:** Mileages are approximate.
**Length:** 30 miles one way
**Directions:** From the intersection of Tanque Verde Road and Catalina Highway (also known as General Hitchcock Highway or Sky Island Scenic Byway) in Tucson, go north on Catalina Highway for 30 miles to Summerhaven.
**Vehicle requirements:** None
**Information:** Santa Catalina Ranger District, 520-749-8700 or www.fs.usda.gov/coronado

# 37

# Pinery Canyon Road

On a late-July morning, my husband picks through a basket of local peaches at the Portal Store while I pore over recent bird sightings. Summer entries are sparse, but two signature species are still among them: the elegant trogon and the Mexican chickadee.

It isn't birds we're after, though. It's the pleasure of a drive through one of the most beautiful and diverse parts of the state. The drive from Portal to State Route 181 in Southeastern Arizona ranges from riparian areas and high-desert grasslands to the pine and fir forests of the stunning Chiricahua Mountains, one of Arizona's "sky islands."

Areas along the drive burned in the Horseshoe 2 Fire of 2011, but even those appear starkly beautiful and serve as a reminder of the resilience of the state's fire-adapted ecosystems.

The air outside feels warm and heavy. We scan the heavens for signs of rain, but the sky is clear and blue except for a single billowy thunderhead, which looks as white and benign as a drift of whipped cream.

Thus reassured, we head southwest on Forest Road 42 and drive into Cave Creek Canyon. The road soon turns to gravel as it runs along Cave Creek in the Coronado National Forest, through a tunnel of overarching oaks and sycamores. Dramatic rhyolite cliffs soar high overhead.

Lush vegetation contrasts with the jagged Chiricahua Mountains, as viewed from Cave Creek Canyon.
📷 RANDY PRENTICE

Sycamores form a canopy over the verdant scenery along Portal Road.
📷 RANDY PRENTICE

A little more than a mile past the Southwestern Research Station, we get our first glimpse of burned hillsides in the distance. As we get closer, the fire's effects appear subtle. Cleared of understory, slightly darkened exposed trunks make the alligator junipers look leggy, with lush grasses carpeting the ground between them.

As the road climbs into stands of ponderosa pines, the effects are more striking, with intermittent patches of blackened trees standing in contrast to a carpet of brilliant green grass, dotted with red penstemon, purple thistle and golden butterweed. In its own way, the effect is dramatic and beautiful.

At Onion Saddle, we take a left at Forest Road 42D for a detour to Barfoot Park, along a road that feels crowded by tall, fire-damaged pines. Not far past a fire-prevention sign, its bright yellow and green contrasting against blackened trunks, Barfoot Park emerges like an oasis, with an untroubled green meadow, a profusion of penstemon blooming from concrete foundations, and a few scattered tents, small and round as the backs of turtles.

A plaque affixed to a boulder notes the park's designation as a National Natural Landmark. Ironically, recognition of the area's unusual mix of Sierra Madre and Rocky Mountain flora was awarded just days after the fire burned much of it.

In contrast, the popular Rustler Park Campground, 2 miles away, remains closed. But the sound of chainsaws emanating from the campground doesn't deter the birds in the day-use area, nor the small group of birders who happily report a cordilleran flycatcher and olive and Grace's warblers.

Back on FR 42, we descend into Pinery Canyon, the pines that inspired its name now resembling a forest of blackened toothpicks in spots, eventually giving way to oaks, junipers and grasslands dotted with century plants.

But by then, our whipped-cream cloud has given way to a dark, threatening sky. Hurrying through some major washes, we startle a deer. Soon, the national forest transitions to private pastures bordered with sunflowers. With relief, we hit the blacktop near the intersection with State Route 181, just as the first drops hit the windshield.

— *Kathy Montgomery*

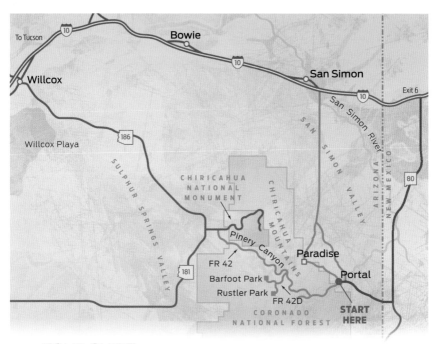

## TOUR GUIDE

**Note:** Mileages are approximate.

**Length:** 24 miles one way

**Directions:** From Tucson, go east on Interstate 10 for 139 miles (you'll cross the New Mexico border) to New Mexico State Road 80. Turn right (south) onto New Mexico SR 80 and continue 28 miles to Portal Road. Turn right onto Portal Road and continue 7 miles to Portal. At the fork, bear left as Portal Road becomes Forest Road 42, then continue 24 miles to State Route 181. For an optional detour, about 12 miles west of Portal, turn left onto Forest Road 42D and continue 2 miles to a fork. The left fork leads 1 mile to Rustler Park, while the right fork leads 1 mile to Barfoot Park.

**Vehicle Requirements:** FR 42 and FR 42D are gravel roads suitable for a two-wheel-drive passenger vehicle, although a high-clearance vehicle is recommended. Open from April through November, these roads are not plowed and are usually closed following early- or late-season snowstorms. These roads are rough and dusty and might be muddy and slick after a rain.

**Information:** Douglas Ranger District, 520-364-3468 or www.fs.usda.gov/coronado

# 38

# Redington Road

**W**ith an afternoon to kill during a visit to Tucson, my husband and I decide to explore Redington Road (Forest Road 371). A popular destination for hikers and off-highway-vehicle enthusiasts, the former military supply route makes a beautiful half-day drive that offers recreation, ranching and history. The graded dirt road winds its way up from the desert east of Tucson between the Santa Catalina and Rincon mountains and through oak- and juniper-dotted grasslands. It tops out over Redington Pass and descends into the San Pedro River Valley and the farming and ranching community of Redington.

We begin on Tanque Verde Road, which becomes Redington Road at its intersection with the Catalina Highway. After about 8 miles, the speed limit drops from 45 mph to 5 mph and cuts through steep switchbacks with sweeping views of Tucson, eventually giving way to a gravel road that is sometimes jarring but manageable in a passenger car.

On this warm Saturday, the first few miles hum with cars, trucks, dirt bikes and ATVs. Just past the pavement's end, parking lots for the Upper and Lower Tanque Verde Falls hiking trails are full. The lower trail leads to a series of pools and waterfalls along Tanque Verde Creek. The upper trail is a 10-minute hike to a swimming spot sometimes used by nude sunbathers.

Below the snow-dusted Santa Catalina Mountains, saguaros and prickly pear cactuses define the scenery along Redington Road.
📷 JACK DYKINGA

Tanque Verde Creek is a popular hiking destination, but beware of flash floods.
📷 RANDY PRENTICE

We pass a large ATV staging area with loading ramps and restrooms at Mile Marker 10. Beyond that, traffic thins, and cars become scarce as prickly pear and ocotillo give way to a rocky landscape covered with straw-colored grasses and dotted with junipers, soaptree yuccas and the occasional corral.

The turnoff to the Bellota Ranch headquarters lies a short distance past the ATV staging area. Pronounced "bay-OH-tah," the historic ranch dates to 1890 and was settled by Henry and Lem Redfield, two brothers from New York who are credited with settling the Redington area in 1875. The Redfields' original adobe house remains on the ranch, as does evidence of even earlier settlers: a pueblo believed to have been built by the Salado people as early as A.D. 1250. Bellota Ranch is now owned by Tanque Verde Ranch. It operated as a guest ranch for a time but is now strictly a cattle ranch.

At around Mile 15, we crest Redington Pass and begin our descent into the San Pedro River Valley. As the high-desert grasslands yield to saguaros, the broad, flat agricultural valley comes into view.

We turn right at Mile Marker 24, where a sign tells us we're 19 miles from San Manuel, and find ourselves on Redfield Canyon Road, where we're surprised by the unexpected sight of a pay phone at the side of the road. We also find the cottonwood-shaded pastures of Carlink Ranch, which is about all that's left of a community that once included a general store, a post office and a one-room schoolhouse. Established in 1884, Carlink is home to the sixth generation of the Smallhouse family, who ask visitors to drive with care.

We return to Redington Road via San Pedro River Road, crossing the dry riverbed over a paved bridge, and get back to town just as groups of off-roaders are packing up. After a pleasant three-hour drive, we, too, feel ready to call it a day.

— *Kathy Montgomery*

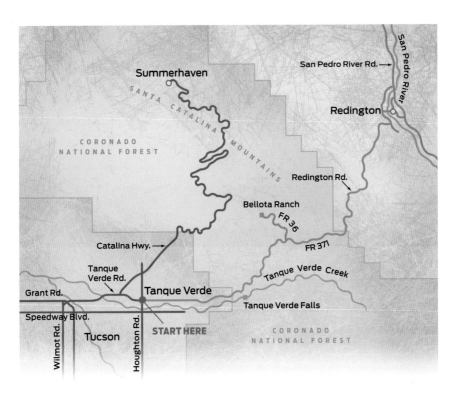

## TOUR GUIDE

**Note:** Mileages are approximate.

**Length:** 62 miles round-trip

**Directions:** From the intersection of Tanque Verde and Houghton roads in Tucson, go east on Tanque Verde Road, which turns into Redington Road, for 28.5 miles to Redfield Canyon Road. Turn right onto Redfield Canyon Road and continue 1 mile to San Pedro River Road. Turn left onto San Pedro River Road and continue 2 miles back to Redington Road. Turn left onto Redington Road and continue 30.5 miles back to Tucson.

**Vehicle requirements:** None

**Information:** Santa Catalina Ranger District, 520-749-8700 or www.fs.usda.gov/coronado

# 39

# Sonoita to Patagonia

On screen, the Sonoita-Patagonia area has doubled as Oklahoma (*Oklahoma!*), Texas (*Red River*) and ancient Israel (*David and Bathsheba*). People claim it looks like Montana, and when you catch glimpses of the vineyards and cypresses, you might reach unconsciously for your Italian phrasebook. But with its pastoral landscapes dotted with pygmy forest and crumbling ghost towns, one thing this region doesn't resemble is the typical coffee-table images of Arizona.

This 56-mile drive begins in Sonoita, headquarters of Southern Arizona's wine country, where you can stock up on a bottle of zinfandel or syrah before venturing south on State Route 83. The winding road is fringed with vineyards, champagne-colored grasses and wildflowers as yellow as the signs warning of cattle crossings and hairpin turns. At 14 miles, one of these turns reveals a jaw-dropping

It's easy to see why the sparsely populated San Rafael Valley has doubled for several other locations in movies.

📷 GEORGE STOCKING

Backlit grass takes on an eerie glow in the San Rafael Valley south of Sonoita.
📷 GEORGE STOCKING

pass where cottonwoods and greenery meander through the fields, backdropped by blue mountains.

But don't be so distracted by the scenery that you miss the turnoff less than a mile later. When you see a sign pointing left to Parker Canyon Lake, veer right instead, down Canelo Pass Road, a.k.a. Forest Road 799. The well-maintained dirt road (suitable for a regular passenger car) winds through a pygmy forest of juniper, oak and maroon-branched manzanita.

At 19 miles, the view opens to reveal the San Rafael Valley — a wide expanse where forest laps up to a savannah smeared with wildflowers. Cottonwoods stand like pins on a map marking the flow of the Santa Cruz River, which trickles from the Patagonia Mountains and Canelo Hills, crossing your path a few times.

Not to toot our own horn, but when Hollywood producer Arthur Hornblow saw a photo of the San Rafael Valley in *Arizona Highways*, he was inspired to set his next film, *Oklahoma!*, here, amid the chest-high, windblown grasses. Then, like now, only a few ranches dotted the land, whereas the Sooner State was too developed to play the role of turn-of-the-century Oklahoma.

The valley has also starred in *McLintock!*, with John Wayne (the scenery must inspire exclamation points); *Tom Horn*, with Steve McQueen; and *Wild Rovers*, with William Holden and Ryan O'Neal.

The road zigzags, but keep following the signs toward Lochiel, a tiny hamlet that spent previous lives as a border-crossing point and a smelter site for neighboring mines. Just past Lochiel, a 25-foot-tall cross commemorates Franciscan friar Fray Marcos de Niza, who entered Arizona on April 12, 1539, to become, the inscription claims, the first European west of the Rockies.

Four miles later, turn left down a somewhat rough road (still suitable for most passenger vehicles) toward the ghost town of Duquesne, pronounced du-CANE. The historic mining outpost consists of five decaying buildings built in the late 1800s, one of which was the home of George Westinghouse, of the electric-company family. Shortly after, you'll pass the blink-and-you-miss-it ex-mining town of Washington Camp.

Two miles later, turn right toward Patagonia onto Forest Road 49, which twizzles through the oaks and sycamores of Coronado National Forest to emerge at views of mauve and coral mountains.

The drive ends in lush and charming Patagonia, where you can refuel with pizza at the Velvet Elvis or picnic at the Patagonia-Sonoita Creek Preserve, a Nature Conservancy-owned bastion for 300 bird species, including gray hawks, green kingfishers and violet-crowned hummingbirds. As you follow the trail along the green and fluttering riverbank, you'll feel like you're in yet another world. Or maybe on a Hollywood movie set.

— *Keridwen Cornelius*

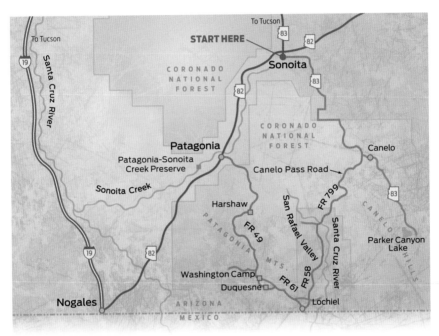

## TOUR GUIDE

**Note:** Mileages are approximate.

**Distance:** 56 miles one way (from Sonoita)

**Directions:** From Tucson, go east on Interstate 10 for 16 miles to State Route 83 (Exit 281). Turn right onto SR 83 and continue 26 miles to Sonoita. From Sonoita, continue 16 miles on SR 83 to Forest Road 799 (Canelo Pass Road). Veer right onto Canelo Pass Road and continue 8 miles to Forest Road 58 (San Rafael Road). Turn left onto FR 58 and continue 9 miles (follow the signs toward Lochiel) to Forest Road 61 (Duquesne Road). Turn right onto FR 61 and continue 4 miles to a rough dirt road that leads through Duquesne. Turn left onto the dirt road and continue 2 miles to Forest Road 49 (Harshaw Road). Turn left onto FR 49 and continue 17 miles to Harshaw and Patagonia.

**Vehicle requirements:** None

**Information:** Sonoita/Patagonia visitors center, 888-794-0060 or patagoniaaz.com

# 40

# Tucson to Buenos Aires

**"G**ood things come to those who wait." It's adage No. 17 in the book of mom proverbs, but in the case of the scenic drive between Tucson and the Buenos Aires National Wildlife Refuge, it is, admittedly, appropriate.

The 134-mile loop begins at Exit 99 on Interstate 19 in Tucson. You'll drive west along the Ajo-Tucson Highway (State Route 86), through the saguaro-speckled foothills west of Tucson proper, before hitting a stretch of level, creosote-capped flatland. Directly ahead, you might notice a dome-topped ridge. The domes house the telescopes of Kitt Peak National Observatory. Cat Mountain looms to the right.

After 21 miles, you'll come to Robles Junction, also known as Three Points. There, you'll turn left (south) onto State Route 286. But be forewarned: Cindy Lou's II Café and the gas station there are the last services until Sasabe, some 46 miles south.

Once you turn onto SR 286, the waiting game turns quickly into a game of I Spy, particularly if you're cruising with someone — maternal or otherwise — who has a keen eye and/or eyes in the back of their head. You'll pass an old VFW post and the Three Points Memorial Park before the buildings move

With Baboquivari Peak in the background, mule deer traverse a meadow at Buenos Aires National Wildlife Refuge.
📷 JACK DYKINGA

Yuccas and mesquite trees dot the grasslands below Baboquivari Peak.
📷 JACK DYKINGA

out of focus and the expanse of the surrounding Altar Valley moves in.

Peppered with mesquite and sitting in the shadow of the Quinlan Mountains, Altar Valley is cut with a patchwork of washes that flow after a heavy rainfall. Baboquivari Peak, sacred in Tohono O'odham teachings as the home of I'itoi, the Creator, is visible to the right. And don't be surprised to spot predatory birds along the route. You might even have to slow down to avoid a gaggle of turkey vultures that have stopped in the road for a midday meal.

The highway enters the Buenos Aires National Wildlife Refuge approximately 20 miles south of Three Points. However, the turnoff for the visitors center is another 17 miles down the paved, easily navigable road. That is where your patience pays off and you can silently thank your mother for a lesson learned.

Established for the protection of the masked bobwhite in 1985, the refuge provides a safe haven for nearly 330 bird species, as well as wolves, foxes, coyotes, cottontails, javelinas and countless Coues deer and mule deer. A glimpse of a doe and her fawn might inspire another quiet thank-you — this time to Mother Nature.

After visiting the refuge, return to SR 286 and backtrack approximately 4 miles to the turnoff for Arivaca Road. The winding, potholed route meanders for 12 miles through wildflower-lined ranchland to the tiny town of Arivaca. Former home to Pima and Tohono O'odham Indians and later settled by the Spanish, the area was known in its early days as L'Aribac, but it was abandoned after an Indian uprising in 1751. Today, small restaurants, a post office and roadside fruit stands lend Arivaca some serious old-school charm.

You'll complete the loop by continuing northeast on Arivaca Road for approximately 23 miles to its junction with Interstate 19 for the return trip to Tucson.

— *Kelly Vaughn Kramer*

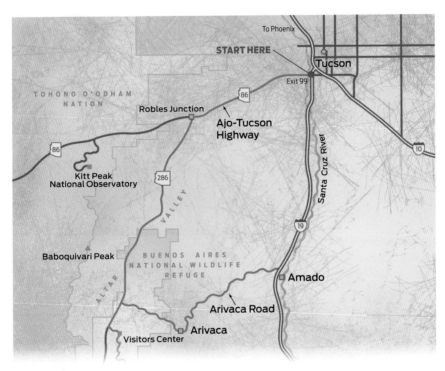

## TOUR GUIDE

**Note:** Mileages are approximate.

**Length:** 134-mile loop

**Directions:** From Exit 99 (Ajo Way) off Interstate 19 in Tucson, go west on State Route 86 (the Ajo-Tucson Highway) for 21 miles to State Route 286. Turn left (south) onto SR 286 and continue 38 miles to the turnoff for Buenos Aires National Wildlife Refuge. Turn left and continue 2 miles to the visitors center. Leaving the visitors center, backtrack 2 miles to SR 286, then go north on SR 286 for 4 miles to Arivaca Road. Turn right onto Arivaca Road and continue 35 miles to I-19. Turn left (north) onto I-19 and continue 32 miles back to Tucson.

**Vehicle requirements:** None; however, roads may not be navigable following a heavy rain. Heed all flash-flood warnings.

**Information:** Buenos Aires National Wildlife Refuge, 520-823-4251 or www.fws.gov/refuge/buenos_aires

# Index

The road to Point Sublime winds through tall aspens.
📷 JEFF KIDA